Alan Titchmarsh
how to garden

Container Gardening

Alan **Titchmarsh**
how to garden

Container Gardening

BBC
BOOKS

Published in 2009 by BBC Books, an imprint of
Ebury Publishing, a Random House Group Company

The Random House Group Limited supports The Forest
Stewardship Council (FSC), the leading international
forest certification organisation. All our titles that are
printed on Greenpeace approved FSC certified paper
carry the FSC logo. Our paper procurement policy can be
found at www.rbooks.co.uk/environment

A CIP catalogue record for this book is available from
the British Library.

ISBN 978 1 84 6073991

Produced by Outhouse!
Shalbourne, Marlborough, Wiltshire SN8 3QJ

BBC BOOKS
COMMISSIONING EDITORS: Lorna Russell, Stuart Cooper
PROJECT EDITOR: Caroline McArthur
PRODUCTION CONTROLLER: Bridget Fish

OUTHOUSE!
CONCEPT DEVELOPMENT & PROJECT MANAGEMENT:
   Elizabeth Mallard-Shaw
CONTRIBUTING EDITOR: Valerie Bradley
PROJECT EDITOR: Polly Boyd
ART DIRECTION: Sharon Cluett, Robin Whitecross
SERIES DESIGN: Sharon Cluett
DESIGNER: Louise Turpin
ILLUSTRATOR: Lizzie Harper

PHOTOGRAPHS by Jonathan Buckley except where
credited otherwise on page 128

Contents

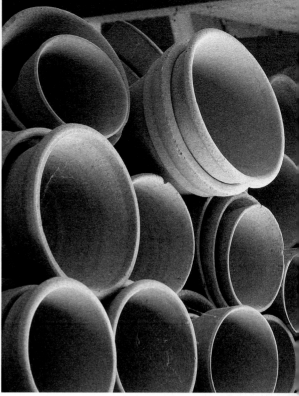

Introduction

Gardening is one of the best and most fulfilling activities on earth, but it can sometimes seem complicated and confusing. The answers to problems can usually be found in books, but big fat gardening books can be rather daunting. Where do you start? How can you find just the information you want without wading through lots of stuff that is not appropriate to your particular problem? Well, a good index is helpful, but sometimes a smaller book devoted to one particular subject fits the bill better – especially if it is reasonably priced and if you have a small garden where you might not be able to fit in everything suggested in a larger volume.

The *How to Garden* books aim to fill that gap – even if sometimes it may be only a small one. They are clearly set out and written, I hope, in a straightforward, easy-to-understand style. I don't see any point in making gardening complicated, when much of it is based on common sense and observation. (All the key techniques are explained and illustrated, and I've included plenty of tips and tricks of the trade.)

There are suggestions on the best plants and the best varieties to grow in particular situations and for a particular effect. I've tried to keep the information crisp and to the point so that you can find what you need quickly and easily and then put your new-found knowledge into practice. Don't worry if you're not familiar with the Latin names of plants. They are there to make sure you can find the plant as it will be labelled in the nursery or garden centre, but where appropriate I have included common names, too. Forgetting a plant's name need not stand in your way when it comes to being able to grow it.

Above all, the *How to Garden* books are designed to fill you with passion and enthusiasm for your garden and all that its creation and care entails, from designing and planting it to maintaining it and enjoying it. For more than fifty years gardening has been my passion, and that initial enthusiasm for watching plants grow, for trying something new and for just being outside pottering has never faded. If anything I am keener on gardening now than I ever was and get more satisfaction from my plants every day. It's not that I am simply a romantic, but rather that I have learned to look for the good in gardens and in plants, and there is lots to be found. Oh, there are times when I fail – when my plants don't grow as well as they should and I need to try harder. But where would I rather be on a sunny day? Nowhere!

The *How to Garden* handbooks will, I hope, allow some of that enthusiasm – childish though it may be – to rub off on you, and the information they contain will, I hope, make you a better gardener, as well as opening your eyes to the magic of plants and flowers.

Introducing containers

Any garden will benefit from the addition of plants growing in pots. They bring colour and interest to any outdoor space, however small, and alongside the ornamental plants you can even create a kitchen garden in a plot the size of a kitchen sink! Containers are frankly indispensable: if you like to ring the changes, you can rearrange everything without having to dig it up first, and you can grow plants that won't thrive in your garden soil (so if you want to grow azaleas, but are stuck with chalky soil, containers are the answer). What's more, with containers you can create a garden from next to nothing.

Choosing the right pot

You can grow plants in practically any container, from a large cooking pot to an old boat. The only requirements are that the container can hold enough compost to meet the plants' needs and that there are drainage holes in the base. But you do need to be aware that some shapes and materials suit certain situations or types of plants better than others.

Containers come in all shapes, sizes, colours and materials. These striking pots, made from coloured concrete, look fabulous in this contemporary garden, but may look out of place in a traditional or rural setting.

The first consideration when you buy a container for a plant has to be the plant itself. Work out how long the plant will be in the pot, because there needs to be enough room for the roots to grow without becoming choked. The container must be stable so it won't fall over in the wind, particularly if the plant is tall. If the plant is likely to need a stake to keep it upright, you'll need sufficiently deep compost to allow for this.

Pot shape

When creating a display, think about the effect you want to achieve and consider the balance of plants in relation to the container. A tall, narrow pot is ideal for a spiky plant or one that can cascade over the sides, but would be inappropriate for a tall, thin plant, which would look top-heavy and precarious. Similarly, a chubby urn suits an unruly mass of foliage, while neat, carpeting plants would make the display look too bottom-heavy. A formal, square planter is ideal for a trimmed, geometric look, such as topiary. A long, rectangular window box or a relatively shallow trough suits smaller plants such as bedding and herbs or alpines, both as a seasonal or a longer-term display.

Consider also the practical aspects of certain container shapes. For example, a pot that tapers towards the top isn't a good choice for permanent plantings, because it can be almost impossible to extract the plant when it comes to repotting and you can damage the rootball. A broad, shallow container poses other problems: the lack of depth means that the plant's roots can't penetrate deep to search for water, and the large surface area provides the opportunity for maximum evaporation of water from the compost. A narrow-based pot would be unsuitable for tall plants (especially in a windy spot) as it would lack stability and may blow over.

Size of container

The size of the container in relation to the plant needs careful consideration. If the pot is too small, the roots will become cramped, which will result in the plant's growth slowing down, drying out and reduced flowering. Conversely, if the pot is too big for the plant, the amount of fertilizer and water in the compost will overwhelm the plant. As you choose your container and the plant to go in it, bear in mind that the plant will grow, so you'll need some idea of the ultimate size of pot the plant will need. The smallest pot you use should be 8–9cm (3–3½in) wide and deep.

If you have a large pot that you want to use but your plant is still small, you can cheat by putting a small pot containing your plant inside the larger one. Simply fill in the rest of the space with compost or an upturned plant pot, or both.

If they're smaller than this they'll dry out frequently. If you're growing a large plant such as a tree, you'll need a container that's about 45cm (18in) across and 30cm (12in) deep. Weight is also an issue: heavy pots are more stable than lighter ones, but they're also more difficult to move around. From a safety point of view, weight is particularly important if your containers are on a balcony or roof (see page 119). You don't want pots to be so light they blow over but on the other hand there may well be weight restrictions.

Materials

When choosing a container, always bear in mind the planting and style of your surroundings. A traditional design calls for classic materials such as stone, while a modern setting requires a contemporary feel, which you can achieve with metal or bright colours for instance. A vibrant planting scheme suits a muted container that will not clash with or distract from the plants. You should also consider the different qualities of the various materials.

Terracotta and glazed earthenware

Traditional terracotta pots look lovely in almost any setting. It's a natural material, so it blends in quickly and ages well. The fact that it's porous means that algae and moss, which live on moisture that seeps through the material, colonize the outer surface, giving the pot an ancient appearance. The main disadvantage of terracotta is that you need to water plants regularly to prevent them from drying out. Glazed earthenware containers are also very attractive and there's a wide choice of colours and designs. They're particularly good where you want to create an Oriental or Mediterranean feel (see pages 12–13). Stand this type of container on pot feet to make sure it has sufficient drainage.

Wood

Troughs, tubs and barrels made of wood all have a natural look and feel that allows them to blend into most informal garden schemes. They're of moderate durability, but last better if you line them with thick plastic sheeting such as a pond liner, or apply a layer of waterproof coating to reduce drying out of the compost. If using plastic, make sure you puncture the sheeting to allow drainage. The main problem, particularly with half-barrels, is that the wood itself must be kept damp. If a barrel dries out, the wood will shrink and the band will fall off, causing the individual pieces to fall apart.

Stone and concrete

Stone is a popular choice for containers, as is reconstituted stone (stone that has been crushed and mixed with cement and then moulded) and concrete, which is sometimes textured. These containers tend to be heavy and traditional in design – ideal for the

A row of vibrant tulips in tall, striking terracotta containers flanks a path that leads up to a front door, offering a cheery welcome and softening the hard lines of the paving. Part of the attraction of this display lies in the repetition of plant and pot.

Don't forget

Not all terracotta or earthenware is frost-proof. Frost can cause the pot to flake or shatter completely, so look for containers with a 'frost-resistant' tag (these may cost slightly more, but will be worth it in the long run).

cottage-garden effect – and are long lasting and wear well. They're not easily moved once they've been planted, so are best used in a permanent position. They usually have good drainage, although they may need to be raised up on blocks or feet. Like terracotta, they lose moisture through the sides, which means that moss and algae will soon build up and give the container an aged effect. You'll have to water regularly in summer.

Metal

Troughs and pots made of metal look particularly good in a contemporary or minimalist setting, where the container is an integral part of the design or needs to be a focal point.

This classic stone urn, with its detailed ornamentation, is offset perfectly by the simple planting: a red-leaved phormium, which provides height and structure, and pretty, small-flowered daisies.

The weight varies depending on the style of the container, but some can be quite heavy.

The big disadvantage of metal is that it does not fare well in a sunny situation, where the container quickly heats up and damages the roots inside. It's possible to get round this by plunging the plant (still inside another container) into damp compost or shredded bark in the metal pot. The material surrounding the plant's pot then acts as insulation against the heat.

Plastic and resin

Plastic pots come in all shapes and sizes and are very flexible, because you can drill as many drainage holes as you want in the base, paint the outside to match your colour scheme, or give the pot a metallic finish so you can enjoy the appearance of metal without the disadvantages. Plastic pots are useful where you may want to change the display regularly, because they're light enough to move around without too much trouble. The disadvantage of plastic is that it will eventually discolour and go brittle, especially if positioned in direct sun. Also, the sides of plastic pots are thin and offer the roots little protection from winter cold. Black plastic absorbs heat, which can damage the plant's roots in summer.

Resin is incredibly light (about the same weight as plastic) but looks very convincingly like stone, pottery, wood or whatever else it's been designed to resemble. Pots made of resin are resistant to frost and heat, and they're easy to drill into when it comes to creating drainage holes.

The beauty of this combination lies in the contrast in form and texture between the tall, sleek metal pot and the tufted grass. Also, the cool, grey and bluish tones create a contemporary, minimalist feel.

Improvised containers

Architectural salvage yards are a wonderful source of interesting materials and unusual containers – chimney pots, for instance, are ideal for trailing plants (see page 19), and clay drainage pipes are perfect for alpines and herbs, especially invasive ones like mint. You can choose a container to fit in with your personality or design. If you're a keen gardener, you might want to plant up an old watering can. If you like fishing or sailing, or live near the sea, there are all sorts of things from small boats to lobster pots that you could use, although they may need lining with plastic sheeting so that they can hold compost.

Oriental style

Two main types of Oriental garden have made their way to the West: the gravel or sand garden (where the landscape is created in miniature using pebbles, sand and minimal planting, adorned with simple ornaments), and the tea garden (where plants in different shades of green predominate). Wood, bamboo, stones and attractive foliage are recurring themes in both types.

Creating a gravel garden can be great fun. As long as you stick to the main principles – minimal planting and simple ornamentation – you can let your imagination go. Start by creating your miniature landscape, using pebbles to represent rivers for example, and then enhance this landscape with your chosen plants and ornaments. Bonsai trees – which are, by definition, miniaturized – are ideal for this style of garden.

Oriental-style plants

In most Oriental gardens, water is an essential element. In the tea garden, low, wide containers of still water can be placed where they will reflect either light or a particularly attractive plant. Japanese maples (*Acer japonicum* and

A. palmatum cultivars) – in green, red or gold – are perfect for this. Other plants include both deciduous and evergreen forms of azaleas for their glorious display of flowers, the black bamboo (*Phyllostachys nigra*), *Pieris japonica*, with its salmon-coloured new growth in spring, heavenly bamboo (*Nandina domestica* 'Firepower') and the slow-growing, multi-branched dwarf pine, *Pinus mugo*. Most of these plants like some shade, so the tea garden is best in a partially shaded area.

For either style of garden, choose plants for their shape because they will be seen in isolation and appreciated from all around, rather than being only a small part of a mass planting. Being so conspicuous also means that the health

of the plants is critical, and they should be fed and watered regularly to maintain peak condition.

If you want an Oriental feel without having to create a dedicated garden, place pots on wooden decking adorned with pebbles and install bamboo screening behind them. Wooden containers give the most authentic effect, especially when they're painted black. White pebbles or plain green moss used as a mulch will complement the dark pots without detracting from the plants.

Oriental-style plants combine with other elements to create a calm, meditative feel.
① A blue-glazed containerized water feature is offset by a bamboo screen.
② A handsome black bamboo looks fitting in a bamboo container.

Mediterranean style

The key to Mediterranean style is vibrant colour. Choose terracotta and ceramic containers and fill them with bright, sun-loving plants. To enhance the effect you can paint surrounding walls or fences in Provençal blue, olive green or bright white.

When it comes to choosing containers, you could use a few large, striking tubs or group lots of smaller ones. In the Mediterranean, it's quite common to see a pot of cascading red-flowered pelargoniums on each step of a flight of stairs leading up to an apartment. The planting can be as mixed as you like, to provide anything from a low-level effect to an all-round design with climbers adding the extra dimension of height.

You could grow a grape vine (*Vitis vinifera*) against a warm wall (or over a pergola to give some shade) and a fig, olive or citrus tree in a large ceramic tub. Other trees that make a bold statement in large pots include *Lagerstroemia*, *Acacia* and *Albizia*; many shrubs are also suitable, such as bottlebrushes (*Callistemon*), hebes, myrtle (*Myrtus communis*) and *Lantana camara*. Cordylines make striking foliage plants, and to introduce colour over summer, try cannas, sunflowers (*Helianthus annuus*), gazanias, tobacco plants (*Nicotiana*), pelargoniums and verbenas. Many herbs have their origins in Mediterranean regions, including oregano, basil, bay, thyme and rosemary, so they will thrive in a hot spot.

Cultivation

Many Mediterranean plants have adaptations that allow them to survive and grow even when water is in short supply and temperatures are high. The leaves are often small (the smaller surface area means they require less water), sometimes covered in tiny moisture-retaining hairs, and they're often silver in colour to reflect rather than absorb light. Many have succulent foliage or stems

that store water. Mediterranean plants therefore thrive in a sunny site, and for many sharp drainage is essential because they can't tolerate sitting with their roots in water. In containers, this means that you need to mix grit into standard compost to open it up and speed the passage of water. For some plants, including lavender and rosemary, this is vital. In cold or damp winters, you may also need to move some plants under cover. If you're planting an area that's hot in summer but may be subject to frost in winter, and you can't keep the plants indoors, use annuals that will die off in late autumn anyway, or take cuttings to keep inside in small pots that take up less room than larger plants.

Bold forms and/or a blaze of colour are both typical of Mediterranean style.
① A few bold, architectural container plants look stunning in a white courtyard.
② Lots of small pots, all containing the same flowers, can be very eye-catching.

Using containers

Containers of all types are ideal for creating a movable feast of colour. Plants can be brought forward as they come into their prime and then moved back to recover once their period of interest is over. These seasonal plants may form the whole display or you could group them around a few permanent evergreen plants, which act as a foil to the changing colours.

Patio displays

This is one of the most popular places for containers, bringing the garden closer to the house and enlivening stark expanses of paving slabs. You may want to follow a certain theme and use containers of the same material. For instance, to create a cottage-garden feel

(see page 19) you could use traditional terracotta pots in different sizes: these will blend naturally into the garden setting without making more of a statement than the plants inside them.

Alternatively, you may want to have the containers play a key role in the display – they may be bold in colour or design, or may be made from a distinctive material, such as metal. If you're opting for a varied, changing, seasonal display, make sure that the pots you're planning to

use aren't so large or heavy that they can't be moved around the garden; bear in mind that compost and water add greatly to the weight. Probably the most commonly used plants for a rotating display are spring bulbs (see pages 88–90 and 107), which look wonderful while in bloom but can get untidy as they die down. Once the flowers have passed their best, the pots can simply be moved to an out-of-the-way area for the leaves to die down naturally, nourishing the bulbs for next year's display.

Hanging gardens

A hanging basket or wall planter is an excellent way to liven up a blank wall, create a welcoming reception by the door or simply extend your gardening area (see pages 34–6). You can choose to tie it into the overall theme of the garden or take

A collection of foliage plants can be just as decorative as a flowering display. Here, lush greens are set off beautifully by deep purples and light, shimmery or soft, silver-leaved plants.

the opportunity to use a burst of colour wherever it's needed.

A traditional hanging basket contains a mixture of species, including tall, bushy and trailing plants in several colours. Today, there is more of a preference for single varieties of plants, in one colour or a mixture. The advantage of this is that you know all the plants inside the basket have the same needs and preferences in terms of light, watering and feeding. It makes looking after it a lot easier.

Hanging baskets vary from open wire constructions to rigid plastic shapes. If you use one with open sides a good liner is essential. Traditionally, baskets were lined with naturally occurring sphagnum moss, but because moss needs to be conserved, a pre-formed, shaped insert or other liner is preferable (*see* pages 34–5). There are also plastic baskets available, with an external saucer attached underneath to catch excess water and provide a supply of moisture for the roots; the disadvantage of these solid constructions is that you can't plant through the sides.

Table and window displays

Window boxes are ideal for adding an extra growing area close to the house where space is limited, particularly where there isn't a garden. Use smaller plants such as summer bedding or alpines for such displays. You can also create your own herb garden in a window box or in pots on the windowsill. The attraction of growing herbs in this way is that they're close at hand: you can pick them fresh, without having to trudge down the garden in the

This pretty display features small pots of white and grey-green foliage plants, including pelargoniums, echeverias, gauras and dianthus.

rain. In addition to their culinary and medicinal uses, herbs (in particular thyme) are often very fragrant and the scent will drift in through the open window in summer; basil is reputed to deter flies from entering the room.

Wood and plastic are the most common materials for window boxes and both can look very attractive. Plastic is easier to maintain, and wood really needs lining with plastic (with drainage holes) to prevent the moisture from causing rot. Watering and feeding are vital to keep the plants growing and healthy in such a small amount of compost. The watering will be particularly important if the box is in a sunny, south-facing site. Before planting a window box, make sure you'll be able to open the window easily once the box is in position and that the box is safely attached so there is no chance that it will fall.

An arrangement of smaller containers on a table on a patio, terrace or balcony means you can enjoy a constantly changing display of single, good specimens or groups of attractive plants closer to eye level. If you move the table close to a window, you can enjoy the display without even having to go outside. Low, alpine-type plants, pretty grasses (*see* page 24), succulents (*see* page 47), very small shrubby plants or dwarf bulbs (*see* page 37) are all ideal for planting in shallow, wide containers or matching pots. You can liven up the display by adding pebbles, larger rocks or even seashells to the containers.

Don't forget

It's best to fill hanging baskets or wall planters when the plants are young, especially if you want to grow some of them through the sides. The main difficulty with growing plants in this way is that the compost dries out quickly, particularly when exposed to wind and sun, so they need lots of watering.

A welcoming entrance

If you have the space – and provided it's not going to become a safety hazard – a healthy container of plants or a collection of plants is a really welcoming sight beside the door, particularly if you don't have a front garden. Plants add colour and interest to the doorway, as well as softening the hard lines of the building and paving.

At the back of the house, a container by the door brings the garden right up to the house itself and provides a display that can be appreciated even on cold or wet days. Spring bulbs are a good example of this, because pots full of bright flowers always lift the spirits and you can place them where you can see them from indoors without going outside into the cold.

Screens and windbreaks

Patios are not always as private or sheltered as you'd like them to be. Your seating area may be over-looked by neighbours, or it may be in the line of a draught blowing round the side of the building. This means that for at least part of the year you may want to screen the patio so you can sunbathe or eat in comfort and privacy.

Containers are ideal for providing a screen or a windbreak (*see* pages 117–19) – they can be placed so that the plants block the eye-line or disrupt the airflow without creating a solid barrier, like a hedge. They're also more flexible, as you can move them around according to your needs (mounting big containers on castors makes them easier to move). It could be that you need the screen in one place if you're sitting or lying down relaxing, but in another if you're at the table eating, so moving the screen will give you flexibility and double the coverage. If you're creating a screen around a balcony, roof garden or other exposed site, you'll need to use plants that will withstand wind (*see* page 118).

A bright display of summer-flowering plants grouped around a front door is a lovely way to greet guests. At the end of the season, the pots can be moved to a less conspicuous spot and replaced with others in their prime.

Balconies are often edged with railings that you can see through when you're sitting indoors. The trouble with seeing out is that other people can see in, and there are times when you might prefer a little more privacy. Much will depend on the type of railing, because the more ornamental it is, the less you'll want to obscure it completely or overwhelm it with too fussy a planting. Trailing flowering climbers across a railing will help create some privacy without forming a heavy barrier. It may be possible to install a mesh screening material inside the railings to screen the view and keep out the prevailing wind, or to fix a small trough to the top of the railing and grow trailing plants that drape down to the ground.

Pots in borders

There are several good reasons for planting a container in a garden border, even though it might not initially seem the most obvious place to put one. First, it's a good way to control the growth of a plant that might otherwise grow too large for your garden: the container will restrict the plant's roots and therefore the top-growth, keeping the whole plant considerably smaller than if it were planted in the border, where it would have a lot of space to grow.

A tiny urban courtyard has been transformed into a private, leafy oasis. Every inch of space has been used – large pots are filled with brugmansia and palms, and a clematis cascades over the trellis.

Another advantage is that you can use a container to add height to the border without using a really tall plant. It provides interest, adds a further dimension to the planting and can make the border seem longer, drawing the eye to a point beyond. You can either bury it partway in the soil or stand it on a single slab set on the soil surface to lift it higher.

Finally, plunging a container plant into a border is a good way to help it survive a dry spell. If you're going on holiday in summer, try planting your pots to about half their depth in the garden soil. The lower temperature will keep the pot cooler and neighbouring plants will shade the container, slowing down the rate of evaporation from the compost. The compost can also establish a capillary link with the soil beneath so that it can draw moisture up from within the soil to help the plant survive.

Unsightly spots

Most of us have an awkward, shady, paved corner by the house, shed or garage. Container plants can bring cheer to these dark, gloomy situations and really make a difference to your living space. It's vital to choose plants that can withstand the shade (*see* page 121). As a rule of thumb, the darker green the leaf the more the plant can tolerate low light levels. Conversely, pale, silvery leaves – for example those of many Mediterranean plants – are usually a sign that the plant prefers full sun. If your shady corner is really dark, or is windswept as well (*see* pages 117–18), it's a good idea to keep two containers planted up – put one on display and move the other to a brighter spot so it can recuperate. Remember, you can make an area appear lighter by painting surrounding walls or fences white or another light colour and by using pale gravel or paving. You could also fix an outdoor mirror nearby to reflect what little light there is (*see* page 123).

A tiny, narrow passageway has been transformed into a lush jungle. The walls, which have been painted white to reflect light, provide shelter for these exotic container plants.

Passageways are common problem areas – they tend to be confined and draughty and may also lack light. In this situation, long, narrow troughs are ideal because they don't take up much space across the width. If you want to cover a wall, the container will have to be deep enough to accommodate the root system of a permanent plant.

There are very few properties without at least one unsightly manhole in the garden. They're large and unattractive yet we have to have access to them, so the best we can do is disguise them. It's particularly important in this situation to consider the weight of the container when it's full of compost: you don't want to break the manhole cover and you need to ensure that you'll be able to lift the container easily – it will be too late to find out that you can't shift it if you have a drainage problem! Rectangular troughs are available that have been designed to cover the average manhole cover

completely, and these are ideal for planting with small, alpine-type plants. However, any round, oval or square container will do the job or else a collection of smaller pots.

Water features

It's perfectly possible to have a complete water feature within a container, from a still pool with a single water lily to a tiny bubbling fountain. The sound of water is pleasantly relaxing and therapeutic and adds interest to the area, however small it may be. You can convert a large ceramic pot or metal container into a water feature by plugging the drainage hole and painting the inner surface with a waterproof coating or lining it with a pond liner; a wooden half-barrel also makes an attractive water feature (*see* pages 40–1).

Cottage gardens and potagers

The term 'cottage garden' brings to mind a pretty little cottage (probably thatched) in the country, with climbing plants rambling round the door and a jumble of flowers in the garden. Many plants that create this cottage-garden effect grow happily in containers, where they can provide a spectacular display throughout the summer.

A woody shrub or climber, such as a rose, clematis or wisteria, can form the basic structural framework of this display. To this you could add annual climbers, such as Spanish flags (*Ipomoea lobata*) and sweet peas (*Lathyrus odoratus*), and other annual plants including argyranthemums, verbenas and gazanias – all of these will provide a mass of colour and flower throughout summer.

The potager takes the theme further by introducing vegetables into the mix. This is the old idea of a kitchen garden, where a small plot of land would supply fruit, vegetables and herbs for cooking as well as flowers for the house. If you want to try this idea, you'll probably need several seed catalogues to help you seek out the ornamental forms of vegetables such as Swiss chard, beetroot, peas and beans.

Sowing seed and cultivation

Many annuals dislike being moved, so it's best to sow the seed into the containers and just let the plants grow *in situ*. You can sow single varieties or a mixture, but be careful not to sow too thickly, which will lead to overcrowding problems and the likelihood of fungal diseases. As an added bonus, many seed-grown annuals produce enough seed themselves for you to save for next year's sowing.

Once the plants are growing, keep them well watered and regularly dead-head the blooms throughout the summer to keep them flowering. Once they begin to set seed, flower production will decline; if you want to keep some seed for the following year, let the seedpods develop (*see* pages 109, 112–13), but be prepared for flowering to slacken off. If you don't want to save any seed, remove the seedheads to keep the plant producing flowers for longer. Flowers need moderate feeding but vegetables are greedier. (For further information on vegetables and fruit in pots, *see* pages 96–8.)

Containers and supports

Terracotta and stone pots look fitting in a cottage-style garden; terracotta-coloured plastic will do too, as the pots will soon disappear under the foliage. If you grow taller plants such as sweet peas or runner beans, they'll need supporting; to continue with the rustic theme, try to use supports made of a material that will blend in, such as a willow or hazel wigwam.

This is not low-maintenance gardening, but the rewards will be huge as you look out over your home-grown display.

Terracotta lends itself to the cottage-garden style as it looks natural, blends into the surroundings and ages well.
① Old chimney pots make perfect improvised containers when filled with flowers such as these pelargoniums.
② A potager in a large terracotta tub contains lettuce, courgettes and sweet peas for cutting.

Planning and designing

Spend a little time thinking about what effect you'd like to create with your containers and what you're hoping to achieve. Just as you consider colour schemes and other design elements in the home, so you should give some thought to the garden before you get planting. Position containers where they can be most enjoyed and where they're easy to water and maintain.

Containers are frequently used as key focal points in the garden – they're designed to encourage you outdoors, highlight a particular location or distract the eye from a less attractive feature near by. In a minimalist garden, a single planted container may be the main feature. A particularly distinctive container will certainly draw the eye, or the planting itself can be the chief attraction. For the latter, plants need to be bold and bright, either in a single colour, in complementary colours, or in a brilliant mixture of hues. Some plants have a distinctive pattern of growth that makes them architectural, others put on a fantastic show of flowers.

Optical illusions

If your garden is fairly short, you can deceive the eye and make the viewer think it's longer than it is by using progressively smaller containers as you go away from the house. Fill them with small-leaved plants that produce small flowers in pale colours and preferably a few that have misty flower stems that are more difficult to focus on. Plants that fade into the distance make the garden appear longer. Large pots of bold foliage and flowers in strong colours shorten the visual effect, so are best used close to the house or window. Height in the foreground also makes the garden seem longer.

Harmony and rhythm

To create a sense of harmony, try to use the same type or colour of pot throughout the area rather than a hotchpotch of styles – green plastic, terracotta and metal will just look messy together. Repetition of plants and containers through the design will give a sense of rhythm – an underlying theme that makes the whole design work. This may be a series of pelargoniums in pots up a flight of steps or the repeated use of plain green plants, which may also serve as a foil for the more colourful ones. In the garden, this task is done by a lawn, which balances the areas of colour and gives the eye a period of rest before the next burst of interest. In a large display, balance areas of bright colour by a similar-sized area of green.

Like a terrace of beautifully designed, identical houses, repetition and uniformity can work very well in the garden. Here, pelargoniums in tall terracotta pots are interspersed at regular intervals by low troughs of mind-your-own-business.

There are all sorts of ways to create a contemporary feel in a garden: with particular materials, colours, shapes, lighting, and of course plants – or any combination of these.

Contemporary design changes all the time, but there are some recurrent themes: modern materials, minimalist planting and bold and/or dramatic colour. There have been many 'black' plants introduced to meet this demand (although most are actually very dark green or red) and they look stunning in silver, bronze or white containers. The range of weather-resistant paints is also increasing steadily and there should be a colour to complement any scheme.

The importance of shape

Form is an essential element of contemporary style. Bold, sculptural planting in large containers instantly gives a modern feel. Palms and palm-like plants such as the Chusan palm

Dark-leaved plants

Aeonium 'Zwartkop'
Alternanthera dentata 'Purple Knight'
Anthriscus sylvestris 'Ravenswing' (black Queen Anne's lace)
Begonia × *tuberhybrida* 'Mocca' series
Capsicum annuum 'Black Pearl'
Heuchera 'Obsidian'
Heuchera villosa 'Palace Purple'
Iresine herbstii 'Purple Lady'
Lychnis × *haageana* 'Lumina Bronze Leaf' series
Ophiopogon planiscapus 'Nigrescens'
Pelargonium 'Bull's Eye' series
Pennisetum glaucum 'Purple Baron'
Pennisetum glaucum 'Purple Majesty'
Salvia lyrata 'Purple Knockout' (syn. 'Purple Volcano')
Sambucus nigra 'Eva' (elder)
Solenostemon scutellarioides 'Chocolate Mint' (coleus)

(*Trachycarpus fortunei*) are ideal for this, as are the Japanese maples, silver birch (*Betula pendula*), the dogwood *Cornus kousa*, contorted hazel (*Corylus avellana* 'Contorta') and magnolias. For a uniform effect you can use topiary such as box (*Buxus*). To soften the edges of severely shaped containers, grasses are effective (*see* page 24).

Effective lighting

Good lighting will bring a container display to life at night. You can use uplighting beneath a well-shaped plant such as a Japanese maple to show off the intricate branches and leaves, or downlighting to give an effect like moonlight falling on a collection of plants beneath. If you have a containerized water feature, you can use lighting to highlight reflections or movement of the water. Light can be set within the water itself or near by, to shine onto it. Solar power makes lighting within plants much easier, because there is no restriction on where the lights can be placed as long as the panel gets enough light during the day to recharge.

Outdoor lighting from mains electricity should always be installed by a qualified electrician, and must be completely waterproof.

To achieve a contemporary look, use containers and plants that are simple, strong in form and architectural.
① Conical containers filled with hostas are striking and unusual.
② A red-leaved phormium, *Phormium tenax* 'Dazzler', set in a tall, concrete pot, makes a strong focal point.
③ Galvanized-steel containers with inset lights planted with *Imperata cylindrica*.

Grouping containers

Containers work well when they're grouped together. From an aesthetic point of view, the grouping is like an over-sized container, allowing you to select both flowering and foliage varieties that will complement each other. Evergreen plants can act as permanent fixtures in the grouping and you can move seasonal, flowering plants into the group as they come into their prime and out again as they start to fade and lose their attraction.

Groups of containers give maximum diversity – you can include seasonal and permanent plantings in the display and a vast range of shapes, sizes, colours and textures.

As well as looking attractive, standing groups of containers close together has a practical benefit because it reduces moisture loss and therefore the need for watering. This is because the leaves form layers that trap moisture underneath and create a more humid environment for all the plants in the group.

Year-round and transient displays

It's important to work out when you want the display to look good. If you want to admire it all year round, the display will need to contain evergreen plants to form a framework that other, more transient plants can be built around.

Flowering bulbs will give a burst of colour from midwinter through to mid-spring. In summer, you can use bedding plants, climbers, summer bulbs, shrubs and perennials. In autumn, fill pots with perennials, late bulbs and corms, and plants for autumn colour or berries. Over winter, opt for winter-flowering shrubs, hellebores and structural plants, which look particularly striking covered with frost or snow.

By hiding smaller spring bulbs underneath your winter bedding, you can have a change in the display without any extra work. The bulbs will come up and flower just as the winter display starts to look tired.

Deep-purple petunias, white daisies, trailing *Convolvulus sabatius* and soft, grey-green foliage combine to create a restful display that has a soothing effect on the senses. The pale clay pot complements the understated arrangement perfectly.

A fiery grouping of red-hot flowers, black foliage and spiky architectural foliage in vibrant pots immediately grabs attention.

Colour schemes

One of the major considerations of choosing plants for containers is colour, so always give some thought to the effect or mood you want to create when planning a display. Flower colour is obviously a key element of seasonal planting schemes, but foliage is extremely important too – it provides a useful foil to set off other plants and can in some cases be the main attraction.

For a bright, attention-grabbing display, select plants at the hot end of the colour spectrum: reds, oranges, yellows, pinks and reddish purple. These vibrant colours look good in pots that are warm and muted in colour, such as terracotta, browns or yellows. Alternatively, if you're feeling brave, go for pots in a contrasting colour, such as a deep blue or green. For a highly modern,

minimalist planting, opt for a shiny metallic container, such as burnished copper. Remember, you can tire of hot, exciting colours so they're probably better for seasonal rather than longer-term displays.

If you intend to create a peaceful area in which to unwind, choose plants in relaxing colours – blues, mauve, blue-purple, pale pink, white and lemon yellow are all calming. Combine them with green foliage plants, such as hostas, or white-variegated plants if you want to lift the scheme. Blue, white, silver, dark-brown or green containers will complete the cool effect.

Plants with gold, silver, bronze or even purple leaves are ideal for creating a metallic effect in a modern setting and you can team them up with either matching or contrasting containers.

A white and green combination looks fresh and clean and is easy to live with. White flowers are superb for shady areas, as they stand out.

Shape and texture

When planning container displays, make sure you consider the different shapes and textures of plants. All too often these are overlooked in favour of colour, yet they're just as important, particularly in long-term planting schemes, which rely more on interesting structure and attractive foliage than on flowers.

There's a huge diversity of plant shapes, and it's good to include a mixture in any planting scheme. Start with vertical or upright plants, for example those with tall spires of flowers or spiky foliage. For contrast, include softer, more rounded forms and those with a more spreading or trailing habit, to cascade down the sides of the pot.

Also, opt for a variety of leaf shapes – wide, rounded leaves give a full, blowsy effect, slender ones add a counterpoint and dissected, ferny foliage can be intricate and elegant.

Texture is also very important, and again, leaves provide the wherewithal to make a display visually interesting as well as tactile. The variety of leaf textures is seemingly endless – smooth and glossy, matt and hairy, leathery, waxy, woolly, feathery, papery, silky and many more. Textured leaves reflect light in different ways, so this adds to the interest.

Using grasses

Grasses are the ultimate 'shape and texture' plants and look wonderful in containers. They form a diverse group of deciduous and evergreen annuals and perennials and encompass little spiky grasses, tall, graceful spikes that wave in the breeze and soft, thin leaves that create a wispy, ethereal effect. Colours include blues, silver-greys and golds as well as green. There are also many variegated grasses.

In a mixed planting, grasses make great 'softeners' among other plants, especially those with finer foliage. They are also lovely when grown on their own as specimen plants in attractive containers. Grasses that produce tall flower stems create a misty effect that makes you look through them to the area beyond.

There is a grass for every situation apart from deep shade, since most originate in open areas with at least some sunshine.

Grasses for containers

Briza media (quaking grass)
Carex 'Amazon Mist' (sedge)
Corynephorus canescens 'Spiky Blue'
Eragrostis elliottii 'Wind Dancer' (love grass)
Festuca glauca (blue fescue)
Festuca valesiaca var. *glaucantha*
Juncus inflexus (rush)
Koeleria glauca (glaucous hair grass)
Lagurus ovatus (hare's tail)
Melica transsilvanica 'Red Spire'
Stipa gigantea (golden oat)
Stipa tenuissima

The most successful container plantings frequently include strong, upright forms and interesting leaf shapes.
① A striking group of grasses and other spiky-leaved plants.
② The spiral, shimmery, metallic green and silver foliage of *Begonia rex* provides the main point of interest in this display.

Scent has the power to take us anywhere and to any time in our past. A smell can evoke a long-forgotten memory and bring to mind someone you love. Without fragrance, the garden is missing a trick. Scented plants are ideal for containers, since you can move them where you can most enjoy their perfume.

Fragrance varies widely, from bold and heavy to light and subtle. Your preference may change from season to season: you might prefer light and fresh in summer, when there are many competing scents, and you may opt for a heavier, more intense fragrance that will hang in the air in winter. There are many clearly identified perfume groups: heavy (strong and long lasting, such as lily); aromatic (spicy scents that resemble cloves or cinnamon); violet (sweet, such as acacia); rose (sweetly fruity, as per roses and some pelargoniums); lemon (tangy, like the leaves of some pelargoniums); fruit-scented (philadelphus); honey-scented (sweet and musky, for instance honeysuckle or buddleia) and animal-scented (musky and less pleasant, such as crown imperials, *Fritillaria imperialis*).

Generally, white flowers tend to have the strongest scent. The reason for this is that pollinating insects are often attracted to plants by their colour; because white flowers lack colour, they need to attract insects in other ways, so draw attention to themselves by their alluring fragrance.

The root, bark, seeds or leaves of a plant may also be fragrant. Aromatic plants are often used fresh or dried in cooking or in herbal teas, or may be used to flavour oils or potpourri.

Positioning the pots
Planning where to put your most fragrant plants is important. If a winter-flowering plant has been put at the back of a border, you're unlikely to cross the wet garden to smell it, so position it near a pathway or window, so you have ready access. Honeysuckle is at its most fragrant on a summer's evening, so it's ideal near a bedroom window or patio door that will be open when the flowers are at their best. Stimulating smells such as those of aromatic herbs (*see* pages 99–100) are best placed near an alfresco dining area, to create a lively atmosphere while you socialize. Calming scents like roses and lavender are enjoyed around the seat where you relax in the evening, to help you unwind.

There are plenty of fragrant plants that look wonderful in containers.
① *Lilium* 'Ebony' is a beautiful dark-flowered lily.
② *Lonicera periclymenum* 'Belgica' has a heady, honeysuckle fragrance.
③ *Lilium* 'Casa Blanca' is pure white.
④ *Lavandula dentata* is scented and compact – an ideal plant for the patio.

Planting and growing

The key to success when it comes to container gardening is to familiarize yourself with the needs of the plant or group of plants you're planning to grow and to create the conditions that match their requirements. Remember that a container plant is completely isolated from its natural growing environment, so it depends on you to provide as good a substitute as possible and to provide for all its day-to-day needs, including food and water. This section shows you how best to do this so that your container plants thrive.

Adaptations to container growing

Unlike plants that grow in the open ground, plants growing in containers cannot fend for themselves. They will do their best to adapt to the restricted conditions, but they will need a considerable amount of help and encouragement from you. Understanding how plants respond to the environment of a pot can help you to provide them with the best possible care and attention.

The root system

During periods of low rainfall or low food supply, a plant growing in the open ground will send sensitive root-tips out or down deep into the soil in search of what it needs. However, a plant in confinement – stuck in a pot in other words – can't do this. Instead, it will make the best of its restricted situation by creating a mass of fibrous surface roots that circle the pot (rather than strong, deep-reaching roots). The fine, fibrous rootball of a container-grown plant is effective at taking prompt advantage of whatever food and moisture becomes available but is not so effective at retaining it. This is why you should water thoroughly – and often – to ensure the roots never dry out. If a container plant does dry out, it can sometimes be revived by plunging it in water, but the chances are that it will have suffered, at the very least, a severe check to its growth. The lack of strong, deep-reaching roots also has an adverse effect on the plant's stability. This is why it's important to choose the right

Summer bedding plants flower more prolifically in a container than in the ground – this is a positive reaction to being 'stressed', or confined in a pot.

pot for the plant: it's not just a matter of aesthetics. A top-heavy, deep-rooting plant will require a far larger pot than a compact, shallow-rooting one of similar size (*see* pages 9–10).

The canopy effect

Outdoor containers do receive rainfall, but the amount of rain that actually falls on the compost is limited. This is because the plant's leaf canopy acts like an umbrella over the compost surface, and much of the rain that does fall is shed over the sides of the pot. While the container-grown plant will have adapted its roots to benefit from any water that does happen to fall on the compost, it cannot entirely overcome this canopy effect. This is the reason why it's important to water container plants carefully onto the compost rather than giving them a light sprinkling from above using a watering can with the rose attachment fitted (*see* pages 46–7).

Flowering

When a plant is grown in a pot, lack of water, food or growing space can result in its becoming 'stressed'. This can lead to poor flowering, pale leaves and stunted growth. However, in many situations, subjecting a plant to stress can actually cause an increase in flower production. This is because if the plant thinks it's about to die, it will 'panic' and divert its energy into rapidly producing more flowers – which in turn release seeds to ensure the survival of the species. This panic flowering effect works for a brief period only, but it's a big bonus in the case of summer bedding, where the display can be magnificent in a small pot if the plants are given enough water and food to keep them going until the end of the season.

Composts and additives

When potting or repotting a plant always use fresh, sterile potting compost. Garden soil should never be used: it compacts easily, offers poor drainage, contains insufficient nutrients and might harbour pests, diseases and weeds. Home-made compost from your compost heap is not recommended either – unless the composting process was very efficient, weeds and diseases may still be present. A specially formulated compost provides a much better growing medium for containers. There are two main types: loam-based and loamless composts.

If you love rhododendrons but can't grow them in the garden as the soil's too alkaline, simply plant them in a pot of ericaceous compost and use rainwater instead of tap water.

Loam-based composts

For plants that are going to stay in the same container for a few years, a loam-based compost (also called soil-based) will be your first choice because it retains both water and nutrients well. The most commonly available loam-based composts are John Innes formulations. All of these are based on a standard recipe and contain 7 parts sterilized loam, 3 parts peat and 2 parts sharp sand mixed with general fertilizer and a little lime. The composts are numbered 1 to 3 (often abbreviated to JIP1, JIP2 and JIP3), each containing increasing amounts of fertilizer; the one you use depends on whether you're potting small, medium or large plants.

John Innes No. 1 Ideal for fine-rooted, slow-growing plants (for example alpines) and young plants.

John Innes No. 2 A multipurpose mix that is good for permanent plantings of average vigour (except acid-lovers).

John Innes No. 3 For permanent large, vigorous plantings such as trees, larger shrubs, climbers, fruit and tomatoes, all of which benefit from the added nutrients.

Ericaceous compost Made without lime for those plants that require an acidic growing medium, such as rhododendrons, azaleas, camellias and pieris.

Loamless composts

A loamless (or soilless) compost is an ideal growing medium for plants that will be in containers for only a few months, such as seedlings and spring and summer bedding. It often holds more water than a loam-based compost, so makes a good choice for small containers, hanging baskets and window boxes, which dry out quickly, particularly in summer. Also, it's lighter and cleaner than loam-based composts, making it easy to handle and a better option for large pots (which will be easier to move) and balconies (where weight may be an issue). Traditionally, a loamless compost was peat-based. However, for environmental reasons peat-substitutes based on other natural materials, such as coir (coconut husk) or composted bark, are preferable. If allowed to dry out, a loamless compost is difficult to re-wet, so it's important to keep it

My own preference is to mix equal parts of loam-based compost and loamless compost to produce a mix that combines weight and nutrient retention with a more open texture.

moist at all times. Also, loamless composts do not hold as many nutrients as loam-based composts, so you'll need to feed the plants more often.

There are three main types of loamless compost available:

Multipurpose compost
The most widely used type of compost, this is a general formulation that is good for general short-term potting, for young seedlings or cuttings, for houseplants that need repotting frequently and for summer bedding containers and hanging baskets.

Seed and cutting compost
This is light and open, enabling the tender young roots to grow easily. It contains a little nutrition to see the plant through its early days but not too much or it could burn the roots.

Bulb compost
This also has a light, open texture. However, it contains little or no nutrition because the bulb doesn't need any until it's dying down, when you have to apply it separately.

Compost additives
There are various specialist products you can add to the compost at the planting stage to improve conditions in the container. You'll be rewarded with longer-lasting, healthier plants.

Controlled-release fertilizer
This releases food into the compost gradually. It usually comes as small, resin-coated pellets that begin to work once they're in a moist environment. Ideally, they need to stay dark and damp to continue

working, although they're also affected by temperature and stop releasing food if it's cold (there is no need for them to work in winter). They can last from 3 to 24 months.

Water-retaining crystals
These are very useful in summer, when plenty of water is needed but may be in short supply. On a hot day, a hanging basket in a sunny spot may need watering twice a day to stop the plants wilting. If you're out at work, this will be difficult, so using these in the compost provides a buffer to see them through. The tiny crystals absorb water and swell to many times their original size. They then release the water slowly back into the compost as it's needed.

Water-retaining crystals, which should be added at the planting stage, greatly reduce the amount of watering required in summer. Add water to the crystals before you put them into the compost. If you put them in afterwards, the compost comes erupting out of the container like a volcano as the crystals swell.

It's well worth adding grit or sand to a container of compost if the plants you're intending to grow require excellent drainage.

Grit and sand
These are good for plants that require free drainage. Both are heavy materials, so they also provide stability to the container. However, they contain no nutrients, so you will have to feed more often to compensate.

Perlite
This can be used in place of sand or grit and consists of light, white granules that are sterile and durable. Perlite helps with drainage, aeration, moisture retention and insulation. Add about 20–25 per cent perlite in the compost mix.

Vermiculite
This naturally occurring, sterile material helps to improve aeration and drainage. It also absorbs nutrients, preventing them from being washed out, and then releases them as required. Add around 20 per cent vermiculite by volume to the compost. The disadvantage of vermiculite is that it has a pH of 7–8, making it unsuitable for ericaceous plants.

A layer of mulch placed over the top of the compost after planting serves several purposes: it reduces the amount of moisture lost to evaporation, so stops the compost from drying out too quickly; it helps to prevent weed seeds from germinating; and – as long as the depth is sufficient (approximately 5–7cm/2–3in) – it stops vine weevils from laying their eggs in the surface of the compost.

There are various toppings available and you can choose one to match the situation and design. Visually, a mulch adds something because it can complement the colour scheme and, if a pale-coloured or reflective material is used, it can help to increase light levels around the lower part of the plant.

Gravel

Long lasting and easy to use, gravel shows off plants well and is available in a range of colours to complement pot, plant or house. However, it tends to sink into the soil so you'll need to top up occasionally. Gravel should be well washed before you use it, as it can be quite alkaline.

Slate

The cool grey-blue colour of slate makes it ideal for a relaxing planting scheme. It usually comes as small, flat chips which lie neatly on the surface, but like gravel it's a loose material and so it can go everywhere if the pot falls over or if you water with a hose.

Bark

This is light, natural and easy to apply but, if it dries out, individual pieces can be blown off the container. Small creatures can also easily burrow their way through it. Bark can be acidic, so it's better used for topping acid-loving plants such as rhododendrons, azaleas, camellias and pieris.

Glass pebbles

These are good at reflecting light, so are especially useful for plants in dark spots, and they look handsome in a modern setting.

Don't forget

Toppings will prevent you from seeing if the compost is moist. You'll have to feel through it with your fingers to tell.

Cocoa shells

Clean and easy to work with, cocoa shells are also lightweight and smell delicious. However, don't use them if you have pets, particularly dogs, because they contain theobromine, which can be highly toxic if ingested.

Weed-proof fabric

This is hardly attractive, and it does need anchoring firmly, but it is very good at stopping weeds, and adult vine weevils can't lay eggs through it. To improve its appearance, cover it up with one of the other materials described here.

Natural toppings come in many forms and can be decorative as well as practical.
① Gravel and larger pebbles combine well or can be used on their own.
② Shells make a good improvised topping, particularly for coastal gardens.
③ Slate is striking in minimalist displays.

Preparing for planting

Give your plants the best possible start by spending a bit of time preparing the pot properly for planting. Before reusing any pot, dispose of all old compost as it may harbour pests, diseases or moss, which will survive to infect the new compost. Then give it a good scrub in water laced with mild disinfectant.

At the nursery, the plants you buy will have been grown on until they reach a good size for sale; in most cases, the rootball just about fills the pot it's in, which means that you'll probably have to repot it fairly quickly.

Tools

A few simple tools are all you need for planting and maintaining your container plants (*see* box, right).

To keep your tools in good working order, make sure you clean them thoroughly after use, particularly if they've been in contact with plant sap, as they can discolour and rust if left dirty. At least once a year, it's worth doing a maintenance check to see if wooden handles have been damaged; they may need sanding down to remove splintered wood. You can rub wooden tools over with linseed oil and wipe an oily cloth over the metal blades or prongs to protect them. If you use a watering can or trigger sprayer to apply fertilizer or chemicals, make sure they're washed out thoroughly before the next use so that there's no chance of contamination.

Providing drainage

Holes in the container base are essential in order to prevent the plant's roots from sitting in wet compost, which makes them soggy and causes them to rot. The number of drainage holes required increases with the size of the pot. Generally, you need 2.5cm (1in) diameter of drainage hole for every 30cm (12in) diameter of compost surface. Good drainage is especially important when growing herbs (*see* pages 99–100) or alpines, which dislike sitting in water.

Compost can sometimes clog single holes and prevent water from getting through. To prevent this, gardeners often put crocks (broken flowerpots) into clay pots before planting. This can provide a perfect hideaway for adult vine weevils to occupy during the daytime, leaving them free to climb the plant and feast at night. They then lay their eggs in the upper layer of compost and the hatching larvae eat the roots. To prevent this, lay a piece of fine mesh across the base of the pot before putting in crocks and compost; a pair of old tights or a small piece of newspaper, cut to shape, will do just as well. As an added precaution, stand pots on pot feet to keep holes from clogging with garden debris. If weight is an issue, you could use polystyrene packing chips instead of crocks.

If the container is made of wood, you'll need to use waterproof paint or line the inside with plastic to protect the wood from rot. Puncture holes in the plastic to allow excess water to drain.

It pays to wash and disinfect pots at the end of the season. Store them somewhere dry so that they're clean and ready for spring.

Tools for planting

- **SECATEURS**
  For trimming shoots for early training, pruning and taking cuttings

- **LOPPERS**
  For cutting larger, thicker stems

- **GARDENING KNIFE**
  For taking cuttings

- **TROWEL**
  For making planting holes in compost

- **WATERING CAN** (with rose) and **TRIGGER SPRAYER**
  Essential for regular watering of container plants

- **DIBBER**
  For pricking out (planting) seedlings and young plants

- **STIFF BRUSH**
  For getting rid of any residue inside a pot that has been used before

- **HAND FORK**
  For breaking up compacted soil, mixing additives into the compost and dividing and separating plants

- **GLOVES**
  To protect against sharp thorns and keep hands clean

- **DRILL WITH A WIDE BIT**
  For making drainage holes in the bottom of a container (if necessary).

Planting a container

After cleaning the pots and ensuring good drainage, you're ready to plant. Whatever container you're using, with the exception of open-sided hanging baskets (*see* pages 34–6) the basic planting method and principles are generally the same. Always water the plants thoroughly before planting. It's also beneficial to soak porous containers in water.

Bare-root and root-balled plants

Woody plants such as trees, shrubs and climbers are sold in various forms. Bare-root plants are grown in open ground and are lifted without any soil or compost around their roots – roses are often sold like this. Root-balled plants are also grown in open ground but the roots are surrounded by soil when lifted and they're often wrapped in hessian or netting for protection.

When planting a window box, think about viewing the display from inside and outside the house and include a mixture of bushy and trailing plants.

Trees and sometimes shrubs are available in this way. Both bare-root and root-balled plants are normally available in late autumn and winter, when they're lifted from the ground during their period of dormancy. They need planting quickly, before the roots can become damaged.

Container-grown plants

Container-grown plants are the most expensive (and increasingly common) type of plants to buy, but they're also the most reliable. They've spent all their lives in pots and establish more easily than other types because their root systems are more developed. Container-grown specimens may be planted whenever you're ready or when you can see roots coming out of the base of the pot.

Bedding plants may be sold as 'plugs', which have been grown in multi-cell packs or in polystyrene strips. Remove the plants carefully to avoid damaging the roots.

Containerized plants

Containerized plants are started off in the open ground but are later potted up into a container for sale. You can usually tell containerized plants by the fact that the soil falls away when the pot is removed. Treat containerized plants as for bare-root, and plant as soon as you can.

A wheelbarrow is useful for carrying plants to the container for planting. It's best to plant large tubs *in situ* as they can be very heavy once filled.

The permanent container

If you're planning to keep a plant in a container for a long time, your choice of compost and container are particularly important. The compost must be nutrient-rich (*see* pages 28–9) and you need to select a shape that will enable you to remove the plant easily when it comes to repotting. If you intend to use a stake, ensure your chosen container is sufficiently deep to contain it. Follow the basic planting method shown opposite and add a support if the plant needs it (*see* pages 38–9).

For climbers, the planting and staking method depends on the type of plant and its support (*see* page 39). If you intend to grow the plant up trellis that is fixed onto the wall, position the plant slightly off centre in the container, to bring the plant closer to the wall, and begin to train it immediately, tying in all the main stems to form a framework. If you're using a support that will stay in the container, place the plant centrally; if there are several plants, spread them evenly around the pot so that each one has equal access to the support.

If you're using a single stake, position it against the rootball at the planting stage. If you're using a frame, fill the container and firm the compost around the plant, then position the frame over, or next to, the plant. Position the stems against the support and tie them into place.

The seasonal container

If the container is going to be needed for a short period only – for example, a display of summer or winter bedding, spring or summer bulbs, or seasonal herbs – you have a greater selection when it comes to choosing a container, because the plants' roots are unlikely to fill the space in such a short time. Herbs and bedding favour John Innes No. 1, which gives the plants stability and nutrients, and bulbs thrive in bulb compost, but for short-term plantings a general multipurpose compost is perfectly adequate. As with permanent displays, drainage is important (*see* page 31).

Don't forget
The top layer of compost in an established pot plant is likely to contain weed seeds. Before repotting (*see* pages 44–5), carefully scrape the upper surface off the old compost, and discard it. You can replace it with fresh, sterile compost up to the mark of the old compost on the plant's stem.

HOW TO plant a basic container

1 Half fill a clean container with a layer of compost mixed with additives such as water-retaining granules and controlled-release fertilizer. Water the plants.

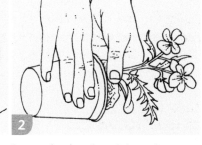

2 Remove the plants from their pots by tapping the pot on a firm edge to free the rootball. If the plant is pot bound, you'll need a little more effort to release it.

3 Gently loosen the roots at the base and at the sides of the plant with your fingers to encourage the roots to grow outwards and downwards.

4 Place the plant on the compost mix to check on the depth. Allow about 1cm (½in) between the plant's 'neck' and the top of the container. Add more compost if needed.

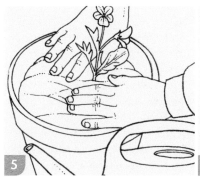

5 Fill around the sides and in between the plants, firming gently as you go. Add more compost until the surface is covered. Water well. You may find that watering makes the compost sink down and you may need to top up or fill gaps with a little more compost.

6 Add a layer of mulch over the surface of the soil to help retain moisture, suppress weeds and keep the roots a little cooler in summer (*see* page 30). Place pot feet underneath the container; keeping the base of the pot off the ground aids drainage and prevents waterlogging.

Planting a hanging basket

The major difference between planting an open-sided hanging basket and other containers is that you can plant through the sides, covering the entire basket with foliage and flowers. Planting can be more fiddly than with other containers, but provided you plant correctly, hang the basket in a sheltered site and water and feed frequently you'll be rewarded with glorious displays in areas that are otherwise frequently neglected.

A pre-formed fibre liner is useful for lining an open-sided basket before planting. Simply pop it into the basket and press it into position.

Types of basket

There are many different types of hanging basket available, from those with solid sides that need no liner to the traditional mesh variety. Open-sided baskets create a lovely all-round effect, as you can plant through the sides in layers as well as at the top. They used to be made of galvanized metal, but today they're usually made of plastic or plastic-covered wire. The disadvantage of open-sided baskets is that moisture can evaporate from the whole surface area, so the compost will dry out quickly and you'll need to water regularly. Also, they're more difficult to plant up than closed-sided ones.

Closed-sided baskets can contain plants only at the top, which means that they're easier to plant up than an open-sided type and no liner is required. Also, closed-sided baskets are easier to water, as they often have a small saucer attached, which means there is a small reservoir. The disadvantage of this type of basket is that you can't create the full, all-round effect possible with an open-sided basket. When planting, remember to use trailing plants that will spill over the sides and cover them, and bear in mind that the plastic may go brittle if the basket is positioned in full sun.

How to plant

The type of hanging basket determines how you plant it. If it's the closed-sided type, you can plant only into the top. These tend to be smaller than other baskets, so opt for smaller plants, including some that will trail down the sides (see opposite). If your basket has open sides, plant through the sides as well as the top (see opposite, far right, and page 36).

You can use multipurpose compost, John Innes No. 1 or a mixture of the two for planting, depending on whether weight is an issue. The multipurpose compost is lighter than John Innes No. 1, but it dries out more quickly and contains fewer nutrients. You can compensate for the loss of moisture with water-retaining crystals (see page 29), but you'll have to feed plants regularly. Water plants well before planting.

Basket liners

A basket liner prevents compost from falling through the mesh in an open-sided basket. It also helps to keep plant roots cool. There's a wide range of lining material available, including pre-formed shapes made of various materials.

Fibre liner This may be made from compressed wood, waste fabric fibres, old wool or coir (coconut husk fibre). It may be pre-formed into a bowl shape that will just drop into your basket, or cut out into a star shape that you press down to fit your basket by overlapping the individual pieces. You can cut your own holes in the fabric for planting through. A fibre liner is inert, so has no effect on nutrition or water retention, and may be dyed green with vegetable dye to make it less noticeable. Some of the coconut fibre liners have a latex coating to help with water retention.

Reduce moisture loss

Moisture is lost very quickly from a hanging basket. You can combat this by placing thin plastic sheeting or a compost bag over the basket liner; then put a plastic plant-pot saucer at the base of the container. This will hold the liner down, prevent water from draining straight out through the base and will act as a water-holding reservoir. Water-retaining crystals will help, too.

An attractive, closed-sided basket contains a bright winter display consisting of skimmia and pansies with ivy trailing down the sides.

For a full, rounded effect such as this you need to use an open-sided basket, where you plant through the sides as well as the top. This glorious, red-themed display makes use of every dimension and includes petunias, verbena, diascia and lobelia.

Compressed paper pulp liner

Made from recycled paper, this type of liner is pre-formed to drop into the basket. It may also have pre-cut holes for planting through. A compressed paper pulp liner is treated to ensure the liner doesn't turn soggy as you water it. It is an inert material, so like a fibre liner has no influence on nutrition or water retention.

Sisal/jute mix liner
This type of liner is either pre-formed or cut into a star shape that you lay in the basket and arrange to fit. Some have a polypropylene backing to help with water retention and they are occasionally coloured green with vegetable dye for moss effect.

Sphagnum moss
A natural material, sphagnum moss has been used for hundreds of years to line planted containers. It has an attractive appearance and excellent water-holding qualities. However, moss is more difficult to work with than a pre-formed liner – it's a loose material and you need to line the basket with a layer of moss about 3cm (1¼in) thick before adding the compost. Avoid using sphagnum moss wherever possible, since the bogs in which it grows need to be conserved.

How many plants?

When planting a hanging basket, you want to achieve a full effect, which may involve including more plants than you think. It's tricky to say exactly how many plants to include in a hanging basket, as it depends on the size of plant, its stage of growth and the style and size of basket. However, as a rule of thumb, if you're using small plants such as strip bedding in a 35cm (14in) open-sided basket, you should include approximately 15 trailing plants (two layers of five through the sides and a row around the top), one dominant central upright plant and perhaps another three to five smaller upright plants.

plant a hanging basket

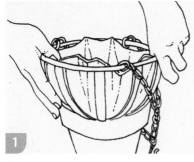

1 Place the hanging basket on an empty flowerpot to keep it steady. Lay the liner in place in the basket, tuck in the folds and press it in position.

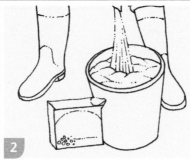

2 Put compost in a bucket and add pre-soaked water-retaining crystals (*see* page 29). Add slow-release fertilizer and mix it all together thoroughly.

3 If the plants are in strips or trays, separate them by pulling them apart carefully. Otherwise, tap the plants out of their pots.

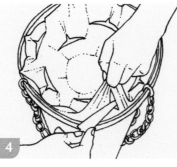

4 To plant through the sides of the basket, make a cut in the liner for each plant using a knife. Add a layer of compost mix.

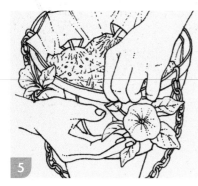

5 Plant through the holes. You can do this from the outside, compressing the rootball of each plant to push it through the gap, or from the inside, carefully feeding the shoots through the hole. Build up another layer of compost around the sides and plant as you go.

6 Place trailing plants around the sides at the top and upright, bushy plants in the centre of the basket. Add more compost, leaving a small depression in the centre of the basket for watering. In summer, water the basket at least once a day and feed approximately once a week.

Hanging the basket

The easiest means of attaching a hanging basket to the wall is a bracket, but it's important to make sure that it's sufficiently strong to take the weight of the basket once it's been filled with compost and plants and watered. Allow time for any adhesive to set before putting any weight on the bracket.

There are rotator devices available, which operate silently by solar power, rotating the basket through 360 degrees to ensure the basket receives an equal amount of light all round. This results in even growth rather than a one-sided effect. Some baskets come complete with a pulley system, which allows you to raise and lower the basket, so you can water and dead-head easily. They operate on a spring-and-ratchet system and some also include a swivel motion so you can rotate the basket.

Evergreen succulents such as these echeverias form a tight globe and make an unusual hanging display.

Bulbs often do better in containers than in the open ground, because they're grown in the perfect medium with good drainage. The main problem with bulbs is the short flowering period, but if you plant carefully you can extend the display time.

Bulbs need planting at different depths, according to their size. Most bulbs should be planted in a depth of soil that is around twice their own height, so a bulb that is 5cm (2in) high needs planting 10cm (4in) deep. Amaryllis and nerines are exceptions, and should be planted with the 'nose' of the bulb just above the soil surface. Cyclamens should be planted with the upper third of the bulb visible above the surface.

For a display that will last several weeks by flowering in succession, plant bulbs at different depths, in layers. Take a large container, add drainage and a layer of compost. First, insert the larger bulbs, such as tulips, then cover them with compost. Next, add a layer of medium bulbs, such as miniature daffodils, cover these with compost, then finally add small bulbs, such as crocuses, snowdrops, grape hyacinths or dwarf irises, and top with a final layer of compost. The crocuses will come up and flower first and then, as they die down, the daffodils should take over. As they fade, the tulips should be getting ready to flower so you will have had colour for much longer than if you just used a single type of bulb in each container. Leave room for an imaginary bulb between each bulb that you plant to prevent overcrowding as they grow.

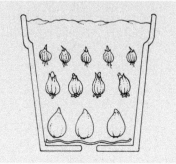

Bulbs provide a splash of colour in spring.
① Tulips and the miniature daisies *Bellis perennis* make a cheery pair.
② Miniature daffodils, crocuses and hyacinths make a pretty, fragrant display.
③ Snake's head fritillaries and plum-coloured pansies are stunning in pink pots.

To plant in layers, insert large bulbs at the base of a pot, then a layer of medium ones, then some smaller ones, with compost between each layer. The bulbs will then flower in succession.

Plant supports

Loose stems that blow around in the wind not only look untidy but they can damage the plant. There are lots of different supports available, from single stakes to obelisks and wigwams. What you use will depend on the plant and the situation. The more functional the support, the earlier you need to put it in place; the foliage will conceal the support in time.

Stakes

When planting a climber or tree it's important to consider whether it will need a stake, because the best time to add the support is at the planting stage. You'll need to make sure the container you choose is sufficiently deep: a container 45cm (18in) wide and 30cm (12in) deep is the minimum size required. The stake should be strong enough to support the weight of the plant until it's stable, so a wall climber may need only a light bamboo cane to guide it into position against the wall, while a tree may need a substantial stake throughout its life. A stake should be tall enough to support the main part of the stem and, if it's a tree, to sit slightly below the lowest branch. If you're staking a flowering plant, the greatest weight will be where the flowers are, so make sure the stake reaches beyond the weak point just below the flowers so you can support the stems. Twining plants can wind around supports without help once they're established, but the support must be no thicker than a pencil or it will be too thick for the plants' tendrils to wrap around.

Planting and tying a stake

Once you have enough compost in the container to set the plant to the correct level, stand the plant in place and position the stake as close to the plant as the rootball will allow. Try to position it so no branches will rub against it. Once you're happy with the arrangement, push the stake to the base of the container for stability and firm the compost around it. You'll then need to attach the plant to the stake. Ties range from simple string for lightweight plants to thick rubber ties for trees. Plastic-coated wire ties need checking regularly, because they begin to bite into the stem if they're too tight. Ties made of self-sticking material are useful, as they can be adjusted easily, but they don't bear great weight, so are suitable only for thinner stems. For trees, use a buckle-and-spacer tie (see below left) to keep the plant from moving in the wind and prevent chafing of the stem.

You can help make a stake more stable by creating an X-shaped frame (see below centre) to sit on the compost surface and brace against the sides. The stake can then be fastened to this to hold it firmly in position.

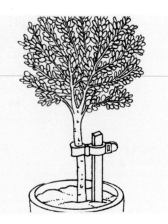

Attach a tree to its stake using an adjustable buckle-and-spacer tie.

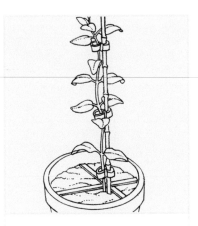

An X-shaped frame provides extra stability for a slender bamboo cane.

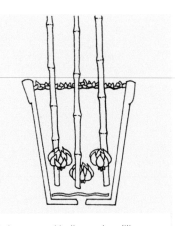

Soft-stemmed bulbs, such as lilies, benefit from staking at planting.

Any soft-stemmed perennials or bulbs that will grow to be tall or floppy, such as lilies, should also be staked at planting (*see* opposite). Carefully push 1.2m (4ft) canes in the compost around the outer edge of the pot, one for each plant or bulb. As the stems grow, tie them to the canes, allowing room for the stem to expand. Alternatively, use link stakes (*see* below). These are L-shaped, plastic-coated metal frames that link together to form a square or circle. Inserting the supports early on means you don't risk damaging the root system and the plants are stabilized from the start. Whether you're using canes or link stakes, the foliage will largely hide the support, leaving the flowers to catch the eye.

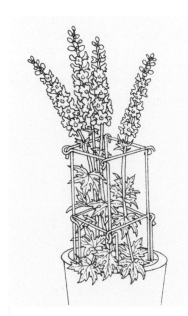

Very tall plants, such as delphiniums, are best supported by link stakes, which provide more stability and allow more natural, spreading growth than individual stakes.

Obelisks and wigwams

An obelisk may be made of metal or wood and is ideal for supporting light, small climbing plants, such as a small-flowered clematis, honeysuckle or rose. With wood you have the option of staining or painting it to tie in with your colour scheme.

A wigwam (*see* right) is similar to an obelisk but less formal. Natural wigwams are usually made of woven willow or hazel stems and suit sweet peas, small-flowered clematis or nasturtiums. You can make your own traditional wigwam out of birch branches, or make a very basic wigwam by spacing three canes around the edge of a pot and tying the tops together with string. Pre-formed metal wigwams can be used in more formal situations.

Whether you're using an obelisk or a wigwam, push the support into the compost at planting so the plants can grow around and over it. The support must be in firmly or it may rock in the wind and loosen the plants' roots.

Trellis

Wooden trellis may be shaped to fit on the container, or it may be attached to the wall behind it. The plant stems can be woven through it, although it's generally a little too thick for the plants to attach themselves to. If you're attaching the trellis to the wall, make sure it's at the correct height and secured at the top and bottom. Position the container as close as possible to the trellis to prevent damage to the stems. You may need to guide the stems to the trellis with a cane.

A wigwam is an ideal way of growing a climber where there isn't wall space for a trellis. Insert it into the compost just after planting.

Check supports regularly

Wall shrubs and climbers need checking regularly to make sure they're tied in to their supports and that the older ties aren't strangling the lower shoots as they expand. Also, check that loose stems can't thrash around in the wind. Make sure that any supports attached to the wall are firmly fixed in place and that any tall or staked plants are protected from high winds.

Don't forget

When fitting trellis to a wall, use long screws with a spacer between the frame and the wall. This allows for air circulation behind the plant, preventing moisture being trapped behind the plant and potentially damaging mortar. It also allows you to feed the stems up behind it, which saves you tying them all in. As they grow, the leaves will eventually hide the frame.

Containerized water features

Water adds a special dimension to the garden – it has a bright, reflective quality when still, and when it flows its sparkling, light-catching surface and soothing sounds bring the garden to life. You can make your own small water feature from any container plus some additional equipment available from your local garden centre. The type of container you use depends on the effect you want to create and your style of garden.

A containerized water feature makes a wonderful focal point in even the smallest garden and deserves to be given a place of importance where it can be admired. However, it's worth bearing in mind that a pond or pool is best positioned where it will get both sun and shade during the day, because too much sun can cause a proliferation of algal growth, while heavy shade will produce spindly plants. If you can, avoid placing the feature too close to deciduous plants, as the falling leaves in autumn can build up in the water and ferment, depleting the oxygen levels.

Even the most basic container such as this half-barrel can be converted into a miniature pond containing plants and fish. It's a great way to encourage wildlife to the garden, too.

Still pool

A still pool in a container is an excellent water feature for a garden of any size. The main advantage of a small containerized pond is that it takes up considerably less space than a regular pond and eliminates the need for excavation work. A container such as a half-barrel is ideal for a still pool, as it has a wide top and sufficient depth to allow planting, but you could also choose a glazed ceramic pot. The minimum size of container required for a small pond is 45cm (18in) across and it should contain at least 23 litres (5 gallons) of water.

Whatever type of container you use, you'll need to ensure any drainage hole is plugged (use silicone sealant or even a piece of cork), then waterproof the inside by lining it with butyl sheeting or applying a couple of coats of a special pond paint. When the paint is thoroughly dry, put the container into place: you can either stand it on a surface or partially bury it under the ground. Half fill the container with water, then let it settle and adjust to the temperature before you add any plants.

For a half-barrel, you can include approximately four submerged plants in baskets and several

Know your water plants

There are four main groups of water plants. Try to include a variety of different types in your container. Note that different water plants need to be planted at different depths.

■ **Deep-water plants** are placed on the bottom of the container; some plants have a minimum depth requirement, so ensure the plant is suitable for the container before buying.

■ **Oxygenators** are submerged beneath the surface; they release oxygen into the water for plants, fish and other pond life.

■ **Marginal plants** are submerged in shallow water at the pond edge.

■ **Floating plants** live at the surface, where they deter algae. They don't need planting in containers.

Many standard water plants can be used in a containerized water feature, but it's best to use smaller species that you don't need to cut back or divide as often. Dwarf water lilies such as *Nymphoides peltata*, *Nymphaea* cultivars, water hyacinths (*Eichhornia crassipes*) and miniature bulrushes (*Typha minima*) are all suitable. (*See also* page 101.)

How to plant in water

Most water plants need to be planted in open-sided, plastic mesh aquatic baskets before putting them into a water-filled container. First, line the basket with hessian to stop the soil being washed out, then add specially formulated aquatic compost. Add the plant or several plants to the basket, then top-dress with a 2.5cm (1in) layer of grit or gravel to stop the surface of the compost being washed away. Place bricks in the container so you can set the baskets at different heights according to the type of plant. Never let water plants dry out.

different types of floating plants. If you intend to add fish, it's vital to include oxygenating plants. These plants can multiply rapidly, so keep them to a minimum and thin them regularly.

Bog garden

A bog garden is an area of constantly wet soil where you can grow moisture-loving (rather than water-dwelling) plants, such as some members of the primula family. It should be sited in a partially shaded area. It is slightly harder work than some of the other features, because once you've installed it, the plants that thrive in these damp conditions really need to be kept constantly supplied with enough water.

Making a bog garden in a container is similar to making a still pool, but there are a few differences. Line a large container, such as a half-barrel, with pond liner. Puncture it to make drainage holes two-thirds of the way up from the base (rather than in the bottom), making holes all the way round. This will allow the upper third to remain slightly drier. The idea is to control the moisture level so that the roots can go down into the wettest soil, but excess moisture can still drain away if you over-water. Fill the container with a loam-based compost such as John Innes No. 1, water well and plant up with bog plants.

A pretty ceramic pot filled with water lilies creates a lovely, Oriental-style feature for summer. Some water lilies are very large, so make sure you choose smaller varieties for containers.

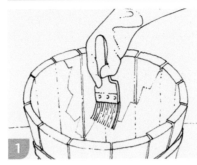

1 Scrape off any loose wood at the bottom of the barrel. Coat the inside of the barrel with pond paint using a paintbrush. Leave the paint to dry, then apply a second coat.

2 Once the paint has dried, place the barrel in its final position – you can partially bury it or stand it on the ground. Half fill the barrel with water using a hose.

3 Plant deep-water plants, marginal plants and submerged oxygenators in mesh aquatic baskets: line the baskets with hessian, fill with aquatic compost, insert the plant or plants into the compost and top-dress with 2.5cm (1in) grit or gravel.

4 Place deep-water plants at the pond base, then create 'shelves' of varying heights for other submerged plants by inserting one or more stacked bricks to suit the different planting depths. Set the plants on the bricks. Finally, add floating plants.

Moving water

The sight and sound of moving water are both highly pleasurable and calming to the senses, particularly on a hot summer's day. A small fountain can look extremely effective in a container and can make a wonderful focal point in a small space – you don't need a lot of room to accommodate one. The depth and shape of the container and the fall of the jet allow for plenty of variation – you can opt for anything from a single jet or multiple heads to a feature that produces a globe shape. The main thing is to keep the fountain in scale with the container.

A bubble fountain is a particularly attractive feature in a small area – water emerges from the pump to bubble up through pebbles or a millstone and disappears into a container again to be recirculated. It gives a soothing sound, is safe for children (as it has no depth of water) and attracts birds and insects to drink.

Siting a fountain

Fountains may be placed above ground within a pot, or may be submerged in an underground container (a central heating tank can be used). You can even set the fountain within a single slab area of the patio or terrace or fix it against a wall with the reservoir or container placed underneath (*see* opposite).

For an above-ground fountain, the container needs to be frost-proof and waterproof. If you have a ceramic container you can use a butyl liner or paint the inside with a silicone sealant. If you use wood,

A fountain in a large terracotta pot, urn or Ali Baba jar, as here, is a handsome feature for a patio. Containers filled with hostas, ferns and bamboos enhance the lush effect.

you'll need to line it or coat the inside with a waterproof paint. There's no need to treat a plastic container at all.

Circulating the water

To get water circulating for a fountain, you'll need a submersible pump. Set the container in position and place a small pump inside, then fill the pot with water. Test the pump and adjust the flow. You can hide the water pipe with attractive pieces of stone in the water.

If installing a fountain in an underground container, dig a hole large enough to sink the tank or reservoir into the ground. Make sure the tank is level, or the water will gradually seep out at one end. Pack under the base of the tank with sand to make it stable. Set the submersible pump in the base, standing it on two bricks to keep it free of sediment. Half fill the tank with water then fill the reservoir to the top.

If you want to make a bubble fountain, place a piece of wire mesh over the top of the pot (or tank or reservoir if it's a submerged fountain) and cover the netting with pebbles. Adjust the flow of the pump so that the water just bubbles up out of the pipe and through the pebbles and falls back down into the reservoir.

Maintenance

You'll need to take the submersible pump indoors in a hard winter, and this is a good time to clean and maintain it ready to use again the following year. A tank set in the ground will need cleaning at least once a year to remove the sediment that settles on the bottom. Top up the container with water if levels become low.

Wall fountains

A wall fountain, which spouts water from the wall into an ornamental container beneath, is a nifty way of introducing moving water into even the tiniest space. The fountain takes up little room and the container or reservoir can be any size or depth, from a shallow bowl to a deep trough. You can buy pre-cast wall features, such as a lion's head or a gargoyle, or you could make your own 'watercourse', mounting a series of pots on the wall in a step-like arrangement, with a spout of water flowing from one container to another.

Don't forget

A containerized water feature is likely to be outdoors all year round, so it will need to be frost-proof. Any container for water will also need insulating against the cold to reduce the chance of the water freezing and damaging the plants (see pages 54–5).

Choosing and installing a fountain

■ Choose containers and fittings that are appropriate for the situation and the scale of the space. A formal fountain with a high jet in a grand urn may suit a good-sized, traditional garden, but will look out of place in a smaller or more contemporary space, where a small, rippling fountain low to the ground may be more appropriate.

■ If children are likely to play near (or in) the water, opt for a feature where the reservoir is covered, such as a bubble or wall fountain. Then they can play with the small jet, but there is no danger of them falling in.

■ If the feature you select needs a pump to circulate water, you'll need an outdoor electricity supply, which is best installed by a qualified electrician.

A lion's head mask spouts water into a generous, solid stone basin. The lion spout is very traditional and the box ball that flanks the trough lends formality to the arrangement.

This eye-catching water feature creates a tranquil haven in the corner of this urban garden. Made from a large wooden trough filled with water and aquatic plants, it incorporates the refreshing sound of running water, fed from a wooden gully above the trough. The blue-green containers and plants provide a harmonious link between the water feature and the rest of the garden.

Repotting

A plant needs repotting if it has been in its container for some time and has outgrown it. The most obvious signs that repotting is necessary are when you see roots coming out of the drainage holes in the container base or at the surface of the compost, the water runs straight out of the bottom of the pot when you water, and the plant seems constantly on the point of wilting.

The plant may also need repotting if the compost lacks nutrients (*see* pages 48–9). The leaves may drop off or change colour to pale green, yellow or brown, flowering and growth may be poor and the plant will eventually die. If you leave it pot bound for too long, the growth will slow right down, and (due to this

When a plant is ready for repotting, squeeze or tap the container to loosen the rootball, place your hand over the compost for support, turn the pot upside down and slip the plant out carefully.

lack of vigour) the plant will become much more susceptible to pests and diseases (*see* pages 56–9). It may have one final burst of flowers in an attempt to make seed that will ensure survival of the species and then it will die.

You can repot plants every year to keep them growing well, ideally in spring as they begin a new surge of growth. Conifers have two growth surges a year, in spring and autumn, and just before either of these is ideal. House and conservatory plants may need repotting more frequently, depending on their rate of growth and how much room you have for them, particularly while they're young. As they age, they will reach their mature size and then grow only very slowly. That doesn't mean that they will not need any more repotting, because they will still use up the nutrients, you just won't need to do it as often.

How to repot

Select a new container that is about 5cm (2in) larger all round the rootball than the old one and fill it with fresh compost. Try to use compost of the same (or similar) material to the existing growing medium (*see* pages 28–9). This will help the plant roots to establish in their new surroundings more quickly.

Camellias are easy to maintain and can live for years in a large pot without being repotted. However, they do benefit from top-dressing with ericaceous compost in spring.

To remove the plant from its existing pot, loosen the roots from the sides of the pot without damaging them. Place your hand over the compost to support the weight, then turn the pot upside down and pull it upwards off the roots. If it won't come off easily, tap the edge of the pot (still inverted) on a surface such as a table very gently. When you repot a conifer, you may see greyish mould around the roots. Don't worry, it's meant to be there. These are 'friendly' fungi called mycorrhizae that live together with the plant in a symbiotic arrangement where both benefit.

If you have a large, heavy pot, lay the container on its side and gently tap the rim of the container with a block of wood, then ease the pot away from the plant. Or, use a hosepipe on a low-pressure setting to wash as much compost as possible out of the container to release the roots, then ease the plant free of the container. If the plant is well and truly wedged in a plastic pot, you may have to cut the pot using scissors. If it's wedged in a terracotta pot, you may have to break the pot to get the plant out, but try washing the roots with a hose first. To repot, plant as you would for a new plant (*see* pages 32–3 and right).

Top-dressing plants

Large patio plants such as trees and shrubs don't need repotting each year (every three years or so will do), but to keep them healthy and encourage flowering it's good to give them a top-dressing annually in spring. Top-dressing is very useful for climbers, which are particularly difficult to repot.

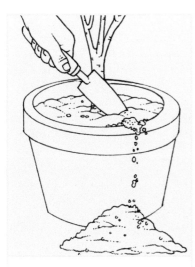

To top-dress a plant, scrape away the upper layer of compost (about 5cm/2in) and replace it with fresh compost that contains slow-release fertilizer. Water thoroughly.

HOW TO repot a container-grown shrub or tree

1 Lay the plant on its side and gently slip the pot away from the plant. If the plant is wedged in firmly, you'll need to loosen the rootball first by tapping the container rim with a block of wood or sliding a long knife between the pot and the compost. Alternatively, use a hose on a low-pressure setting to wash the roots away from the sides of the container.

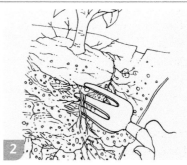

2 You may see a thick coil of roots that form a solid pot shape around the plant, depending on how pot bound it is. Using a hand fork, gently prise the congested roots from the solid mass so that they can grow into the surrounding compost once replanted in the new container. Any thick roots that will make repotting difficult can be shortened.

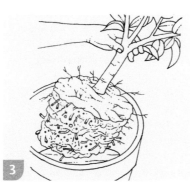

3 Prepare the new, slightly larger pot for planting. Place a layer of mesh then crocks at the base of the pot, covering the drainage hole (*see* page 31), then add a layer of compost to cover. Place the plant in the centre of the pot, spreading out the roots.

4 Fill the gap between the pot and the plant with more compost, firming lightly. When potting is complete, the surface of the rootball should be about 2.5–5cm (1–2in) below the rim of the pot to allow for watering. You can prune the top-growth by about one third (*see* page 51).

Choosing a container

When choosing a new container, aim for a pot that is approximately 5cm (2in) larger all round than the previous one. It may be tempting to go for a very large pot with the idea that it will save your having to repot too often, but it's a false economy – too great a difference between the pots will check the growth of the repotted plant. A quick-growing plant will need moving up every year, usually in spring, but a slower one may need to move up only in alternate years. If you don't repot a plant that year, it will need feeding to make sure it has enough nutrients.

Watering

One of the most important aspects of care with container-grown plants is watering. Plants in containers dry out far quicker than those growing in the open ground because their roots are restricted and can't extend to seek out water in the soil.

Quantity

The amount of water a plant requires depends on a number of factors. Bright sun and wind seem to just suck the moisture from the plants and compost, so you'll need to water more frequently in sunny or exposed areas. If you have a hanging basket with moss sides or a porous container such as a terracotta pot you'll have to replenish water lost through the container's sides and top. Compost is also a key factor: if it's very free draining it means watering more often. Finally, you need to consider the plant itself. Some plants need more moisture than others. Generally, the larger the plant and the larger the surface area of the leaves the more water the plant will require.

You need to keep the compost in the container damp all the way to the bottom, all the time, to ensure that there is always enough water for a plant's demands. Roots cannot survive in dry soil and will die off, reducing the amount of food and water the plant can take up, making it unstable. As an approximate guide, a very large container – such as a half-barrel 1m (40in) in diameter and filled with plants – can use up to 6 litres (1.5 gallons) of water a day in dry weather.

Frequency

Basically, you should water your plants whenever they need it. A small container that is fully planted, such as a hanging basket in a sunny position, may need watering twice a day, while a large container in a partially shaded site may be happy with watering on alternate days. You have to get to know your plants and their requirements and take into account where the pots are placed in the garden. Don't water by the clock.

Hanging baskets need masses of water throughout the summer. To reduce the amount of watering you have to do by hand, install a drip irrigation system. This can be connected to an automatic timing device.

When watering, make sure you soak the compost thoroughly rather than giving just a light sprinkling. The water needs to soak through the compost and reach the plants' roots.

The point of no return

A plant's cells are full of water and depend on it to maintain their structure. Without enough to keep them plumped up, the cells begin to shrink away from their neighbours – we see this as wilting. When the gap between these cells becomes too great to rebuild, it has passed the 'permanent wilting point', which means that even when the plant is watered again it is unlikely to recover.

Plants benefit more from a really thorough soaking than from a short watering that penetrates only the upper layer of compost. The latter encourages all the roots to become concentrated towards the top of the pot, making the plant unstable. As the plant can't take all its needs for a day in one go, water has to be available for as long as possible. There needs to be enough water in the pot for the plant to draw upon as and when it needs it but not so much that the roots sit in water, or they may rot. If you're short of time, or go away in summer, consider fitting an automatic irrigation system that will come on every day. You can install a timer switch and set it to come on overnight. There are also several other things you can do to help your plants survive without you while you're away (*see* page 109).

Timing

The best times to water are in the evening and early morning. If you water in the middle of the day, you are unlikely to do any real harm (in spite of those who suggest that it can cause scorching), but most of the water put on will have evaporated long before the plant can use it. Watering in the evening or early morning, when the air is cooler and the sun is lower, allows time for the water to soak through the compost and reach the roots. Slugs feed at night and can travel around much more easily when there is a film of moisture everywhere. If you water in the evening, be prepared to have slug-control measures in place.

If your plants dry out, most will recover from a brief dry period once they're watered, although the thinner the leaf, the quicker it will reach the point of no return. Check the compost regularly and add a little more water each time until you can see the plant recovering. Little and often is the key. The very worst thing you can do to a dry plant is keep soaking it or leave the roots standing in water for too long, because you simply exchange dehydration for drowning. If the compost is too wet, there is no room for air in it and without air, the roots can't breathe.

Some loamless composts can 'shrink' and be difficult to re-wet once they have dried out. This is one of several reasons why I like to combine loam-based and loamless mixes (*see also* page 28).

If your containers are in an exposed, sunny position you may need to water twice a day in summer. Always water thoroughly.

If you're away a lot, or don't have time to water regularly, choose plants that can get by without you for a while. Succulent plants (above) retain a lot of water in their plump leaves, which means they can survive for longer between waterings.

Feeding

A container plant can survive for some time without feeding, but if left too long the rate of growth and overall health will begin to suffer. It may start to look paler, flower less and produce shorter shoots. If the lack of food continues, the plant will become susceptible to pest and disease attack. Gradually, flowering will stop, growth will slow down and the plant may look yellow and sickly.

Plants in containers need more regular feeding than those in the open ground to keep them healthy and growing vigorously. A general fertilizer is fine for most plants.

What plants need

Plants require a number of minerals and trace elements to grow well. The major nutrients are: nitrogen (N) for shoot and leaf growth; phosphorus (P) for root growth; and potassium (K) for flowers, fruit and winter hardiness. If you look at the back of a fertilizer pack, it should give the N:P:K ratio in the product, which will vary according to the purpose of the feed. Additional major nutrients include magnesium, calcium and sulphur and trace elements such as iron, copper, manganese, boron, zinc and molybdenum.

How much fertilizer you apply and when you start feeding after planting will depend on the compost you used in the container (*see* pages 28–9). Loamless composts normally contain fewer nutrients than loam-based ones, so the plant will need additional food much sooner. On average, you should apply a feed about three or four weeks after planting in loamless compost, because the plants should be growing quickly in their new home and may be very hungry. For plants that need a special boost, you can apply a short course of seaweed-based fertilizer: seaweed is very rich in trace elements and acts like a tonic for an ailing plant (almost as an antibiotic would for humans).

Plants have a natural cycle, with periods of fast growth, slow growth and near-dormancy (they are never entirely dormant). They need the most feeding during the period of active growth, less during the slow growth and none when they are at their slowest. Aim to get into a habit of feeding your container plants once a week during spring and summer, maybe on a particular day so you don't forget. This will help keep the growth rate constant and

If leaves start to look sickly it could well be that the plant is suffering from a nutrient deficiency of some kind. This illustration shows leaves suffering from various common deficiencies, in clockwise order starting from the bottom left: potassium, phosphate, nitrogen, manganese and iron, magnesium.

the plant healthy. Little and often is far better than overdosing them once a month, which will lead to surges of growth, followed by periods of relative inactivity. Nutrients will gradually leach out of the container as you water and especially during periods of heavy rain, so if you notice a change in the colour of the leaves, you may need to increase the feeding for a while.

Fertilizer types

A general fertilizer will contain a balance of the three major nutrients (N, P and K), along with a range of minor nutrients, and is designed to keep most plants healthy. It is ideal for shrubs, trees and other long-term container plantings. However, you may need to correct a nutrient deficiency or promote a certain type of plant growth and this is where specific fertilizers can help. For instance, if you're growing plants such as camellias or azaleas that need acid conditions, you need a fertilizer that contains more iron. These are usually sold as 'ericaceous' or 'acid-loving' formulations.

If you're growing tomatoes, peppers or other fruiting plants, a fertilizer that is high in potassium (K) will help, as it aids the production of flowers, fruit and seeds. A plant that is being grown entirely for its foliage will look better if you apply a feed that is high in nitrogen (N), as this benefits all the top-growth and will improve the colour of the leaves.

There are many different ways in which you can apply fertilizer. It comes in liquid or solid, granular or powder form. Most types are applied to the roots but some are applied to the leaves. Foliar feeds are particularly useful for plants such as bromeliads that cannot absorb fertilizer easily through their roots.

Liquid fertilizer Liquid feeds are easy to use, but some may be washed out of the base of the container along with the excess water. It is usually a ready-to-use concentrated formulation that you dilute to a recommended strength. Pour the appropriate amount of liquid fertilizer into the measure, then add it to the watering can. Fill the can with water, stir the contents with a stick to mix them together and water the plant in the usual way.

Fertilizer sticks and pellets
Fertilizer sticks are simply pushed into the compost and become activated on contact with water, releasing feed gradually into the surrounding soil. Don't push them too close to the roots, or they may cause a localized concentration of

If you don't have time to give your plants a regular liquid feed, you can pop fertilizer sticks into your hanging baskets and other containers in spring. They release fertilizer very slowly as and when it is needed.

A liquid feed that is high in potassium is ideal for tomatoes and other fruiting plants, because it encourages growth of flowers, fruit and seeds. Make sure you use the correct amount stated on the bottle.

food and scorching may occur. Pellets are sprinkled on the surface of the compost.

Soluble powder or crystals
These need to be dissolved in water before application. Measure the crystals or powder into the scoop provided, add to a watering can full of water and stir well until dissolved.

Controlled-release granules or pellets These work continuously and save you having to remember to feed. You need to mix them with the compost before planting. The instructions will normally give a quantity of granules per litre volume of compost, so you'll need a container of a given volume (for example 5 litres) that you can fill with compost.

Don't forget

Always read the instructions on the pack of fertilizer and try to stick to the recommended rates of application – at least until you get to know your plants and their needs.

Pruning

The purpose of pruning is to keep the plant healthy and improve its performance – it encourages growth, boosts flower or fruit production, enhances its shape and restricts the size of the plant. There are entire books dedicated to pruning, and for the novice the subject can seem complex, but pruning needn't be cause for concern if you follow a few simple principles – these are the same whether you're gardening in the open ground or in containers.

Remove individual flowers as they fade. Once a rose has finished flowering, remove 15–23cm (6–9in) of stem together with the dead flowers. Cut the stem just above a leaf joint.

Damaged or diseased stems should always be removed as soon as you notice them. Removal of stems that are weak and spindly will help to improve the overall vigour of the plant. Plants whose stems have become congested will also benefit from a little pruning as this will enhance air circulation round the stems and leaves (which in turn will help to discourage some diseases).

Pruning for performance is all about making a plant do what you want it to do. In most cases it's carried out to increase production of flowers and fruit, so the first thing you need to know is when your plant flowers. Plants tend to set their flower buds weeks, if not months, before they actually open so, if a plant flowers in spring or early summer, pruning in winter or early spring will remove these flower buds and you won't get a display. Camellias, for instance, set their flower buds for spring during the previous summer and autumn. The easiest time to prune safely is just after the plant has flowered, because that gives it a full year to produce the shoots and buds that will flower next year. As plants seldom flower on the same wood twice, it is usually safe to remove the stems bearing the faded flowers so that you encourage new shoots to form lower down. On many shrubs, the older the stems are, the greyer they are in colour. New stems tend to be a lighter brown and any others will be somewhere in between.

Types of pruning

There are various pruning methods. The one you choose depends on the results you're hoping to achieve.

Dead-heading The simplest form of pruning, this involves the removal of dead flowers to

To dead-head camellias, simply pluck off the dead flowerheads when they start to fade and turn brown. This will encourage new buds to form and will also keep the plant looking well groomed.

encourage new buds to form and stop the plant from setting seed. Towards the end of the flowering season, you may choose to leave a few seedheads to form if you want to keep some seed for the following year (see pages 109, 112–13).

Formative pruning This is when you cut back young woody plants after planting. Remove weak or spindly growth and any that has been damaged. If you wish, you can prune the plant further to take the remaining shoots back to a strong bud that faces in the desired direction. This is particularly useful for climbing plants, where you want the shoots to grow towards the wall or support. Cutting a plant back hard will encourage it to produce new shoots from lower down, increasing the overall bushiness and shoot strength, although it is likely to delay flowering.

Remedial pruning This may involve anything from a light trim to a complete overhaul. To keep the plant growing and healthy, you need to apply the 'four Ds' rule at least once every year – remove dead, dying, damaged and diseased shoots completely. Once you've done this, move on to remove any congested, crossing or misshapen shoots. Congested growth reduces the airflow through the plant, which increases the chance of fungal spores settling and taking hold, and crossing shoots are likely to damage themselves as they rub together in the wind (the open wound this creates encourages pests and diseases). If you have variegated plants, remove any shoots that have reverted to green (*see* box, page 52).

Containment This type of pruning is aimed at keeping the plant thriving in its container for as long as possible. Some plants (particularly shrubs) tend to grow vertically and can get too tall for their containers quite quickly. However, by cutting back the tips of the growing shoots (*see* right), you can encourage the buds lower down the stem to open, resulting in a bushier plant that will be suitable for the container for longer. Some plants can be cut back quite hard every year, others resent it, so do some research before you prune.

If you have only limited space, you will eventually reach the point where the containers you're using are as big as you can cope with. At this point, you have to decide whether to get rid of the biggest plants or try to keep them within their pots. One way to do this is to prune the roots. You'll need to get the plant out of the pot and then wash as much soil off the roots as you can. Then, using clean, sharp secateurs, remove about one-third of the roots. This may be complete roots or, in the case of camellias and rhododendrons, a slice (just like a slice of cake from a whole circle, but don't go right up to the stem). This will need doing about every third year. If you have removed a slice, next time make sure you remove a different part of the rootball. Once you've removed the roots, repot the plant back into the container with fresh compost and water well (*see* pages 44–5). The top-growth will slow down as the plant concentrates on replacing the lost roots and the plant will slowly grow to fill the pot.

To keep shrubs and trees in pots in tip-top condition, restrict their size and retain their shape, cut back the tips of the growing shoots. This can be carried out when repotting (*see* page 45).

Hard pruning This can be a good idea when a plant is looking particularly old and tired, or if the shoots are thin and not flowering well; ideally, it will provoke a flush of new shoots. Not every plant will respond to being pruned hard, because it means cutting back into the oldest wood and some will not

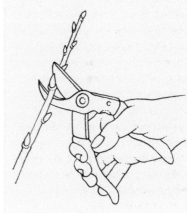

Where a plant has alternate buds, make a diagonal cut just above a bud. The cut should slope down behind the bud.

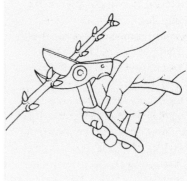

Where the plant has opposite buds, make a horizontal cut straight across the stem, just above a pair of buds.

regrow from this. However, if you have reached the stage where the plant has one last chance before you give up on it, it may be worth having a go.

Hard pruning involves cutting back each stem right down to a few buds at its base in the hope that they, and any dormant buds around the bottom of the stems, will grow. It can be done over several years, rather than in one go, so that it gives the plant less of a shock. One stem in three is often enough to start with, and means that you don't lose the whole plant if it doesn't work. The following year, take out another third, making sure you remove the old stems not the new ones. As the new stems grow, you can pinch the tips out to encourage sideshoots to form and produce a bushy plant if you want to.

Reversion

Plants with variegated leaves (green mixed with paler green, yellow or white) arose as single genetic mutations that were propagated to produce new varieties. The original green form that they sprang from remains in their genetic memory and so occasionally these plants will produce an all-green shoot – this process is known as reversion because the plant is reverting to its original form. Because the variegated leaves contain less chlorophyll (the green pigment that the plant uses to convert sunlight into sugars and starches for energy), the stronger green shoots will grow faster and eventually take over if they are not removed.

Don't forget

The leaves of a plant are its power house, manufacturing food from sunlight to nourish the plant and give it energy. Every time you prune you remove some leaves, so you need to feed the plant to replace the nutrients until it can make its own again.

Topiary

Since the 17th century, possibly earlier, formal, clipped hedging plants have been used as architectural features in the garden. Dense-leaved evergreens such as yew (*Taxus baccata*), box (*Buxus sempervirens*), holly (*Ilex aquifolium*) and privet (*Ligustrum ovalifolium*) lend themselves to tight clipping to train them into neat shapes and are perfect for containers.

True topiary can take a great deal of time. To create and retain the trimmed look the shrub needs clipping two or three times a year during the growing period when young, and once or twice a year when mature. To save time but to create a similar effect, you can use pre-formed meshed wire shapes and plant several shrubs, trees or climbers close together (between two and five depending on their size) in order to fill the shapes more quickly. There's nothing wrong with a little bit of cheating!

Rosemary clipped into a cone in a large terracotta tub makes a handsome, year-round focal point in this courtyard.

There's no end to what you can do with topiary – plants can be clipped into highly ornamental and fantastic shapes. However, simple geometric forms (here, clockwise from bottom, spheres, cones and spirals) frequently work best and are quicker to achieve. If you haven't got the patience to train plants yourself, potted topiary is widely available and although expensive provides instant effect.

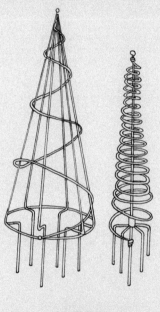

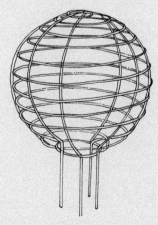

HOW TO clip topiary to shape

Hedging plants of dense growth, such as box, privet or yew, can be clipped to shape as they grow through a pre-formed wire frame.

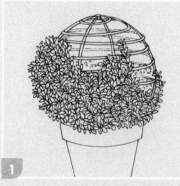

1

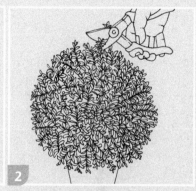

2

Plant dense-leaved plants (here, box) into a large container using a loam-based compost such as John Innes No. 3. Insert the wire frame. As the plants grow, trim to keep them within the confines of the framework, pinching out the growing tips regularly to make the stem produce sideshoots and become bushy.

Once the shape is well filled, simply clip it back into shape with secateurs or shears. Box should be trimmed in late spring, privet twice in summer and yew in late summer. Feed and water the plants well to keep them healthy and watch out for any pests or diseases that will spoil the appearance of the leaves.

HOW TO train climbers for topiary

Climbers such as small-leaved ivies (*Hedera helix*) and creeping fig (*Ficus pumila*) as well as other plants such as myrtle (*Myrtus*), thyme (*Thymus pseudolanuginosus*) and houseleeks (*Sempervivum*) can be trained to grow up wire shapes.

1

2

Plant several plants (here, small-leaved ivies), preferably with long, trailing stems so you can begin training straight away, into a large container of loam-based compost such as John Innes No. 3. Insert a conical wire frame into the compost and tie garden wire around the frame to fill in any large gaps. Train the stems up the framework, tying them loosely in place with string or plastic ties.

Continue tying in the stems as new shoots develop. Once the shape has been filled in, use secateurs to trim off any straggly or unwanted growth. Check the oldest ties regularly to make sure they're not cutting into the stems.

Overwintering

Container plants are particularly vulnerable to cold weather because they're isolated from the insulating properties of garden soil: it's the difference between having a cotton blanket or a feather duvet. If the plants are not frost hardy you'll need to move the containers indoors or lift the plants and pot them up for overwintering indoors. Even hardy plants may need some protection, and if the pots aren't fully frost-proof they will need to be covered or taken indoors.

Pelargoniums, fuchsias and other half-hardy perennials need to be taken indoors over winter. Cut them back to about half their height: this removes leafy growth that might otherwise turn mouldy.

Frost, wind and snow

Frost can kill parts of the plant directly or indirectly. Directly, it causes the outer cells of the plant to freeze solid and split, or the liquid inside the cell to freeze and expand, which we see as a blackening of the shoot tips or new (tender) leaves. Indirectly, it can kill parts of the plant if they cannot thaw gradually. For example, if the early morning sun falls on frosted camellia flowers, the heat causes the cells to rupture as they thaw out too quickly. Frost causes most damage in winter or early spring, when plants have just started into growth.

Strong, cold winds can also cause damage by burning the outer leaves of a plant. The combination of low temperatures and wind speed causes desiccation (drying) because the moisture is being drawn out of the leaves faster than it can be replaced by the roots, which leads to the characteristic brown scorching on the leaf surface. Conifers and broad-leaved evergreens suffer most from drying winds. Shelter is important, so make the most of any that you have by moving the most sensitive plants out of the wind. Buildings can retain heat, as well as offering shelter from wind. The wind chill problem is made worse if the rootball is frozen, because there is water present but in a solid, rather than liquid, form that the plant can't use.

Snow is usually less of a problem than frost and drying winds, because thick snow is a good insulator against the cold. However, the weight can cause branches to fall and plants to split apart, so however pretty it looks, it's worth knocking it off your smaller plants.

It is particularly harmful when the thaw increases its weight and when it re-freezes.

Water

Even in winter, plants need a regular supply of water to stay alive. Long periods of cold can leave plants without adequate water and although their systems can slow right down, the absence of water will eventually kill them. The best approach is to insulate containers to ensure that any water present doesn't freeze.

Conversely, plants will suffer if there is too much water. Inadequate drainage will leave the roots sitting

A young hebe shoot has been damaged by early morning frost in spring. The shoot tips have turned black and the leaves have withered and turned brown.

Don't forget

Plants give off moisture, so never wrap your plants in plastic for longer than a few hours: the plant's moisture will condense on the inside of the plastic and, if the temperatures fall, it will freeze, sticking the leaves to the wrapping and thereby causing more damage than if you had no wrapping there at all.

in sodden compost over winter. Too much water leaves no room for air, and without air, the roots cannot breathe. If the roots cease to function, they will rot and die, and the first you will know about it is in the spring when the leaves open and then die off. Drainage is crucial and to make sure your pots are going to drain properly, you may need to stand them up on bricks or pot feet over winter. If you notice that a pot is full of water, lay it on its side for a day to let it drain out, then stand it up again.

Lifting tender and half-hardy plants

You won't be able to keep tender or half-hardy plants outdoors over winter, because they'll be killed by frost, but you can take them indoors and plant them outdoors the following year. Dig the old plants up in autumn before there's a frost, cut the tops down to about 15cm (6in) and put them in containers in a frost-free greenhouse or conservatory. You can replant them outside again in late spring after risk of frost has passed, usually mid- to late May.

A handsome terracotta urn filled with sculptural grasses and berrying and trailing evergreens – here, *Carex comans*, skimmia and ivy – takes on a beautiful, ethereal quality when rimed with frost.

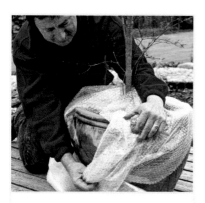

If you're expecting a big freeze, it's well worth insulating your outdoor tubs with bubble wrap, as prolonged periods of frost can kill even fully hardy plants. The compost can be covered for a few days at a time.

Frost-protection materials

In winter, the part of the plant that is most at risk of damage from both wet and cold is the roots, so protecting these should be your main priority. There are various forms of insulation you can apply if you want to leave containers out year round.

BUBBLE WRAP

■ Bubble wrap is useful for insulating around the sides of your containers. You'll need a piece that is long enough to wrap all the way round the pot (once or twice), then simply tie it in place with string. As long as it is not covering the surface of the compost, the bubble wrap can stay in place until the weather warms up a little.

NEWSPAPER

■ Crumpled newspaper is very easy to use as an emergency means of protecting the roots. Simply open out a large plastic bag (a black bin bag is ideal) and stand the container inside. Take single sheets of newspaper and scrunch them loosely, then pack them around the pot until the bag is almost full. Draw the top of the bag together and tie it around the stem of the plant. You can open it up again during the day to allow air to the roots, but don't let the paper get wet.

FLEECE

■ Horticultural fleece is an invaluable weapon against cold in the winter. It's light, folds down quite flat and allows light and air through (so the plant can still photosynthesize and breathe). Draped over the top of a plant it can help withstand several degrees of frost, especially if you use more than one layer. If you realize that your camellia flowers have been hit by frost, you could help prevent damage by putting fleece over the top before the sun hits the blooms.

Plant problems and remedies

All sorts of things can go wrong with plants in containers; the reasons can be lack of care, inclement weather conditions or pests and diseases. The best way to avoid problems is to prevent them from happening in the first place – by keeping plants healthy – but if problems do occur it's much easier to deal with them if you catch them early.

Many of the problems associated with plants can be controlled by taking simple steps to maintain good hygiene. Fungal spores can remain dormant for long periods of time until the conditions they need for growth are right. Microscopic as they are, they may be on the wall, floor or woodwork and on any of the pots, trays or tools that you're using. Similarly, the eggs of insects may remain hidden, waiting for suitable conditions for the larvae to hatch. There are several simple precautions you can take to reduce or even eradicate this threat. First, wash all your pots and trays in a disinfectant solution before you re-use them and clear away old pots and compost before they can attract fungal spores. Cut away any growth that looks damaged before it can infect the rest of the plant or pass to others and remove dead leaves from in and around the containers – this is important all year, but especially in autumn. Wash down the walls around your plants with disinfectant solution in late autumn. If you have a greenhouse, use a citrus-based cleaning solution to clean the walls and floor, paying particular attention to the crevices around the glazing.

Examine plants frequently to see whether watering, feeding, repotting or weeding are necessary, and remember to dead-head and prune as needed. Also, check for pests and diseases and treat the condition promptly if needed. Lift out dead plants straight away and, before replacing them, try to determine the cause of death – if they've been attacked by a soil pest you shouldn't use the same compost for replacement plants.

Common pests

As with plants in the open garden, plants in containers are susceptible to pests. Even plants on a balcony or terrace can fall prey to attack – slugs and snails can travel great distances vertically, as long as the wall is moist, and have been reported as high as a fourth-floor balcony.

Some problems can be lived with, as long as the aesthetic effects of the attack don't bother you. Try to avoid chemical sprays: they're damaging to the environment and, along with the foes that you want to be rid of, they often eradicate friends – the beneficial insects that you want to encourage (see page 58). The development of resistance in some insects also means that chemical controls are not always as effective as you think.

There are now biological controls for many pests (see box, right): these target only the bad guys, so do not adversely affect the beneficial bugs. The great thing about containers is that they provide a limited environment, which is ideal if you want to introduce predators – for

Biological controls

Almost every garden pest has a predator, so once you know the enemy you can release it and hope that it annihilates garden pests on your behalf. Great advances have been made recently in the use of nematodes (microscopic eelworms), predatory insects and selective bacteria that will keep the population of pests under control. These methods of control cause no environmental damage, use no toxic chemicals, are safe around children and pets, are easy to apply and pose no problem with resistance. The only limiting factor is that they need a mild temperature to live and become active, so the treatments don't work outside in winter. Insect predators, such as hoverflies and lacewings (whose larvae feed on aphids), are ideal for use in a greenhouse or enclosed area.

Predators eat the pest (or its eggs or larvae); pathogens infect the pest with a fatal disease; parasites live on (or in) the pest, ultimately killing it; nematodes are parasitic worms.

PEST	BIOLOGICAL CONTROL OR PREDATOR
Aphid	*Aphidius* species (parasitic wasp larva)
Caterpillar	*Bacillus thuringiensis* (pathogenic bacterium)
Mealy bug	*Cryptolaemus montrouzieri* (pathogenic nematode)
Red spider mite	*Phytosieulus persimilis* (predatory mite)
Scale insect	*Metaphycus helvolus* (parasitic wasp)
Slug	*Phasmarhabditis hermaphrodita* (pathogenic nematode)
Vine weevil larva	*Steinernema kraussei* (pathogenic nematode)
Whitefly	*Encarsia formosa* (parasitic wasp)

example eelworms to deal with soil-level pests such as slugs and snails. You simply water on a preparation containing the eelworms (nematodes) and they will do the work for you. Also, many pests can simply be removed by hand – the simplest and often the most effective remedy.

Below are some of the most common garden pests, the problems they cause and recommended treatments to get rid of them.

Ants
Ants can kill plants, not by eating them but by tunnelling along their roots and causing them to dry out. They also like to 'farm' aphids for their honeydew – in effect they are running a protection racket!
Prevention and control The trick is to keep things damp so that they go elsewhere. They also dislike the smell of mint, so planting a low-growing form of it such as pennyroyal (*Mentha pulegium*) can help deter them.

Aphids
The distortion of shoot tips and new leaves is a symptom of aphids. There is also a sticky coating on leaves (honeydew), sometimes with black sooty mould.
Prevention and control Remove and destroy badly infected plants. Catch them early before the populations build up. Spray the foliage with a sharp jet of water, and wipe off any small infestations with your fingers. Organic controls include insecticidal soap (based on fatty acids), derris (derived from tropical plants) and pyrethrum (derived from a type of chrysanthemum). As with many other pest problems, encouraging the pest's predators in the garden is helpful (*see* page 58). Aphid predators include ladybirds, lacewings, wasps, spiders and hoverflies.

Caterpillars
The most obvious signs of caterpillars are holes eaten in leaves, flowers and seedpods. The plant may be completely defoliated.
Prevention and control Remove caterpillars by hand. For large infestations, use a biological control (*see* opposite). You can use this in conjunction with a pheromone trap to let you know when the moths are laying eggs and make the treatment more accurate, as the bacteria have to come into contact with the caterpillars quickly or they will die.

Earwigs
Small, circular notches or holes in leaves and flowers often indicate that earwigs are present on a plant.
Prevention and control You may consider a small amount of damage from earwigs as acceptable, because they do eat aphids, one of the greatest garden pests. However, they can wreak havoc with some types of flower (such as dahlias), in which case you will want to reduce their numbers. A pot filled with shredded paper or straw will serve as a trap as well as an earwig hotel – depending on whether you're trying to catch them or encourage them. Place the stuffed pot upside down on top of a cane and leave it overnight. Adult earwigs will use it as a hide-away. In the morning, you simply empty the trap, or you treat it as a mobile hotel and transfer it to a place where the earwigs can do some good – to an aphid-infested container plant, for example.

Froghoppers
These insects produce clusters of frothy bubbles on stems and leaves, looking like spittle or discarded washing-up water (the bubbles are sometimes known as 'cuckoo spit'). Each cluster conceals the nymph of the froghopper, which as an adult looks like a cross between an aphid and a grasshopper. They do no harm at all, but you may consider the 'spit' aesthetically displeasing.
Prevention and control If you want to get rid of them, you can spray with a jet of water or pick off by hand as soon as they are spotted.

Leaf miners
These cause pale green or white wiggly lines on leaves. They are an aesthetic nuisance rather than harmful.
Prevention and control Pull off affected leaves as soon as they are spotted. Use a biological control if necessary.

Lily beetles
These eat holes in leaves, flowers and seedpods of members of the lily family, from mid-spring to late summer. The plant can be completely defoliated. The black mucky deposits on stems and leaves are the beetle larvae concealed in their own excrement.
Prevention and control Small numbers of plants can be protected by picking the adults and grubs off by hand. You must be vigilant, however: despite their bright red colour, lily beetles are remarkably adept at

avoiding detection. Inspect the plants regularly, picking off the beetles and wiping off the black residue containing the grubs. They overwinter in the soil, so plants that have suffered heavy attack should be repotted into a clean pot with fresh compost.

Red spider mite

Signs of red spider mite are stunted growth, and curled and mottled leaves covered with a fine webbing that protects the breeding colonies. Do not confuse these mites with the small, fast-moving red spiders (which are totally harmless to plants).

Prevention and control Spray the undersides of leaves frequently with water, and maintain high humidity (as they prefer dry conditions). Use a biological control (*see* page 56) or spray with insecticide as soon as the damage is spotted.

Scale insects
Scale insects cause stunted growth and yellowing of leaves. There is a sticky coating on the lower leaves, sometimes with black sooty mould present.

Prevention and control Barrier glue around the stem stops the larval stage moving to new parts of the plant. Apply a biological control in summer (*see* page 56) or an insecticide in late spring or early summer.

Slugs and snails
Overnight, you find that holes have been eaten in plant tissue. Damaged seedlings are usually killed.

Prevention and control Apply a mulch of sharp gravel around the plants as a barrier. Copper bands around pots deliver a small electric shock to these pests, discouraging them from reaching the plant. Beer traps can be effective, but remember to empty them every day. There are also biological controls (*see* page 56).

Vine weevils
The larvae of the vine weevil eat the roots of plants, causing the whole plant to wilt or collapse. Small, semi-circular notches bitten out of the leaf edges are caused by the adults.

Prevention and control Keep the compost surface clear of debris (which can hide adult female insects). Use a thick mulch to stop the female laying eggs in the compost. Apply parasitic nematodes or add insecticide granules to the compost (*see* page 56).

Whitefly
These cause the leaves to develop a yellow, freckled appearance; there is a sticky 'honeydew' (whitefly excrement) on the upper surface of lower leaves and a form of sooty mould.

Prevention and control Use yellow-coloured sticky traps to attract and catch flying adults. Introduce a biological control in summer (*see* page 56) or apply an appropriate insecticide in late spring and early summer.

Beneficial creatures
There are many garden creatures that can help you in the campaign to kill off pests, without you doing a thing other than providing a safe, undisturbed, preferably chemical-free haven in which they can live a quiet life, away from predators. Birds are the great friend of the gardener – you could attract them to your garden by feeding them in winter and providing clean water and shelter in the form of trees and shrubs. Hedgehogs are also helpful – again, provide them with somewhere to shelter: a couple of rotting logs among shrubs is perfect. If you have a pond, you'll encourage frogs and toads, both of which eat pests that live near or on the ground. There are also numerous beneficial insects – ground beetles feed on soil pests, velvet mites eat small insects such as red spider mite, centipedes feast on mites, slugs and other insects, and lacewings, wasps, hoverflies, spiders and ladybirds all devour aphids. Encourage insects to stay in your garden over winter by postponing your autumn tidy up until spring, leaving them with plenty of hiding places.

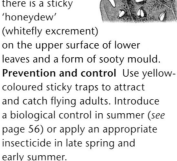

Unwanted visitors
Neither animals nor insects recognize boundaries and if something attracts them, they will investigate it, whether we want them to or not. For some uninvited guests, there are chemical controls that can be used, but there are certain steps we can take to make the garden uninviting without having to resort to this. If you know there are cats in the vicinity, for instance, then don't plant catmint (*Nepeta × faasenii*) that will attract them.

Common diseases

Diseases are caused by bacteria, fungi and viruses. Fungi and bacteria are encouraged by poor weather conditions, while viruses are often transmitted by insect pests. All problems are exacerbated by poor husbandry.

Botrytis
Also known as grey mould, this results in yellowing and browning of leaves. The stems may rot at ground level. The plant becomes covered with a grey, felt-like mould.

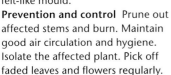

Prevention and control Prune out affected stems and burn. Maintain good air circulation and hygiene. Isolate the affected plant. Pick off faded leaves and flowers regularly.

Canker
Small sunken areas of bark enlarge and restrict growth, leading to stem die-back.
Prevention and control Prune out affected branches or cut out affected area and paint the wounds with copper-based fungicide as soon as symptoms are spotted. Remove and burn badly affected plants.

Coral spot
Individual branches of trees and shrubs wilt in summer and grey-brown staining may be found under the bark. In autumn the dead bark is covered in small, salmon-pink blisters.
Prevention and control Prune to remove affected wood and burn infected material immediately. Prune in summer when there are few fungal spores in the air. Dispose of prunings.

Downy mildew
Discoloured, yellowing leaves have white patches beneath. Plants often die slowly in autumn.
Prevention and control Use disease-resistant cultivars. Avoid overcrowding and maintain good air circulation around containers. Remove and burn badly infected plants.

Fireblight
Flowers and young shoots of trees and shrubs in the Rosaceae family blacken and shrivel. Leaves wilt and turn brown; shoots die back.
Prevention and control Grow as few susceptible plants as possible. Remove and burn any plants with these symptoms.

Powdery mildew
White, floury patches appear on young leaves. Shoots are distorted and there is premature leaf fall.
Prevention and control Keep plants well watered as mildew thrives in dry conditions. Prune out infected stems in autumn to prevent spores overwintering. Spray fungicide on the young leaves (the fungus cannot penetrate old leaves) at the first signs of infection.

Root rot
Foliage turns yellow, branches die back from the tips, and affected roots usually turn black.
Prevention and control Avoid heavy watering and improve drainage. Never use unsterilized compost. Dig up and burn affected plants. Choose varieties known to be tolerant or disease resistant.

Rust
Leaf surface has yellow blotches, the underside has bright orange or brown patches of spores; leaves eventually drop off.
Prevention and control Increase plant spacing to enhance air circulation. Remove all affected parts.

Silver leaf
Leaves of trees (especially *Prunus*) adopt a silvery sheen. Branches die back. Brownish-purple brackets appear on stems.
Prevention and control Prune in summer when there are few fungal spores in the air. Remove infected branches. Badly infected trees must be wholly removed and burned.

Viruses
Foliage is small, distorted, or grouped in rosettes. Leaves develop yellow coloration.
Prevention and control Buy healthy, virus-free plants. Control potential carriers (insect pests) and clear away weeds, which may harbour viruses. Remove and burn affected plants, and do not propagate from them.

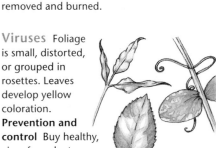

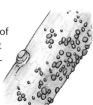

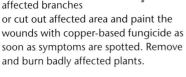

Propagation

There are several very good reasons to have a go at propagating your own plants, not least that you can increase your range of container plants at very little expense. Top of the list of reasons though must be the great satisfaction that is to be had from watching a plant grow that you've sown or rooted yourself.

Methods

There are lots of ways to propagate container plants, using all parts of the plant. Sowing seed is probably the most common way to propagate but other methods include taking cuttings (from the roots, stems, shoots or leaves), dividing plants, and propagating by layering, air layering, grafting or budding. Not all of these are applicable to every plant, and some techniques are much easier than others. Grafting and budding are normally practised only by very experienced growers.

Sowing seed

Seed is easy to sow, usually fairly inexpensive (free if you collect your own, *see* pages 109, 112–13) and you get lots of plants from it. However,

the results aren't always predictable, because of genetic variation, so you may get some plants that are better than the parents and some that are less good.

For the best chances of germination, sow fresh seed if possible. However, some seed can last for a surprisingly long time: poppy seed has been found to be viable after 70 years. If you do store seed, it's best to put it in an airtight glass jar in a dark, cool but frost-free place. The most important factors for seed germination are temperature and moisture. Seed is unlikely to germinate if it's too hot or too cold, or the compost too dry. A germination temperature of 18–21°C (65–70°F) suits most plants.

Seed sizes vary considerably, from the dust-like seeds of some begonias to the coconut. Each will have its own requirements when it comes to germination. Some seeds (particularly trees, shrubs and some alpines) need chilling before they can germinate, so you'll need to put them outdoors over winter or in a refrigerator for six weeks before sowing. Many types of seed need covering with a layer of compost after sowing, while others require exposure to light. You can maintain high humidity around the seeds by putting a sheet of glass or plastic over the seed tray until the seeds have started into growth. Stand seed in good light but not direct sunlight, as the sun may scorch the young shoots. If it's a very bright spot, such as a windowsill, you may have to shade the plants with fine netting.

Each seed has a supply of food inside that is sufficient to keep the seedling alive as it grows up to the light. Planting the seed too deeply means the food will run out before it gets to the surface. Generally, the smaller the seed, the lower the reserves and the nearer the surface it should be sown.

Sowing the seed too thickly or leaving the seedlings in too dark a place will result in them becoming long and straggly.

Some seeds are very fussy about the ambient temperature, requiring it to be within a particular range and constant before they'll deign to show themselves. If you want to grow seed like this, you'll need to invest in a heated propagator. Many seeds, however, are far less particular and will reward you handsomely for what really amounts to very little effort.

Some seeds should be sown beneath the surface of the compost, such as beans (left); others should be scattered over the surface and left uncovered, such as poppy seed (right). If you buy seed, the packet instructions will tell you what to do. If you collect your own seed and have no idea how to sow it, work on the principle that the larger the seed, the deeper it should be sown.

HOW TO sow small seed

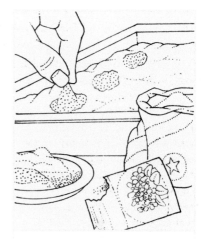

Fill a pot with seed compost and firm it down gently. Scatter the seed onto the compost, ensuring you get a thin, even distribution over the surface. If the seed should be covered, sprinkle over sieved compost until it disappears from view. Then stand the pot in tepid water until moisture has soaked up to the surface.

Place the pot inside a loose plastic bag or a propagator and put it in a light spot but not in direct sunlight. Check daily. If the compost dries out, water again in the same way. When the first seedlings germinate, discard diseased or damaged seedlings. Once the seedlings have opened out the first true leaf, they need transplanting, or 'pricking out'.

Mix very fine seed, such as begonia, with fine sand, then sow it in 'pinches' or scatter it evenly over the surface of the compost. The seed should be evenly distributed through the sand for easy handling. The sand helps you see where you have sown the seed.

HOW TO transplant or 'prick out' seedlings

Fill a clean seed tray with fresh compost and firm it gently. Then take a dibber and use it to gently loosen clumps of seedlings and separate the roots from the compost. Don't handle the stems. Carefully lift each seedling and lower it into a finger-sized hole in the new compost, spacing the seedlings about 3.5cm (1½in) apart.

Ensure the seed leaves rest just above the surface of the compost. Gently firm compost around the seedling to cover the roots and fill the hole. Water them in, either by standing the tray in water or by using a fine rose on a small watering can. Place the seedlings in a bright spot, but out of direct sunlight. Keep the compost moist.

Keep a close eye on their progress and, after six weeks, begin feeding the plants once a week with a general-purpose liquid fertilizer. When the tray is full of roots, the young plants will be ready for potting up into larger pots filled with fresh, sterilized compost, such as John Innes No. 1. Handle the young plants very carefully.

Taking cuttings

Unlike growing plants from seed, propagating from cuttings gives you a predictable result, because the cuttings grow to resemble the parent plant almost exactly. Some may be demanding to root and require a propagator, but many can be rooted in pots. You may have to try several times to establish which type of cuttings works for which plants and the best time of year to take them.

Softwood cuttings

Also called tip or shoot-tip cuttings, these are cuttings of soft, fast-growing new shoots, taken in spring and summer before the growth begins to harden and turn brown and woody. If you haven't grown plants from cuttings before, start with easy ones, such as pelargoniums, osteospermums or fuchsias, as they root easily. Softwood cuttings of most plants will root between spring and early autumn. Fill a 10cm (4in) pot with cutting or seed compost to just below the rim, then prepare your cuttings as shown here.

Pelargoniums are among the easiest plants to propagate from softwood cuttings, ideally taken in summer.

HOW TO propagate softwood cuttings

1 Using a sharp knife, remove lengths of strong, healthy shoot from the plant. (Always take more cuttings than you need in case some don't root.) The best plants for this method are pelargoniums, fuchsias, argyranthemums, penstemons, tender perennials and osteospermums.

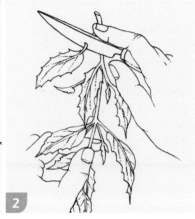

2 Remove the basal leaves from each cutting and trim it just below a leaf joint. For most plants, you should have a cutting of about 8cm (3in) long, with two to three leaves at its tip. (Note that fuchsias should be 2.5–5cm/1–2in.) If necessary, dip the cut stem bases in hormone rooting powder.

3 Using a pencil or thin stick, dib the cutting into damp seed and cutting compost. Don't push the cutting in too far: its remaining leaves should be clear of the compost. By placing cuttings around the edge of a pot, you should be able to fit several cuttings into one pot.

4 Thin-leaved cuttings need humidity. Place a clear plastic bag over the pot and hold it in place with an elastic band (this acts as a mini-greenhouse and keeps the humidity high until the roots form). Once new growth starts (in about four to six weeks), the cutting is ready for potting.

Semi-ripe cuttings Semi-ripe cuttings are best taken in mid- to late summer as the growth begins to harden on the current season's shoots. They're less likely to wilt than softwood cuttings, because they're slightly tougher, but they will take longer to root. Many shrubs, such as camellias and lavender (*Lavandula*), as well as evergreen herbs, conifers, box (*Buxus*) and heathers (*Calluna*), root well when taken this way. Look for young shoots that are just starting to turn brown and woody.

Hardwood cuttings These are taken from growth that is one year old, in autumn or early winter. You can take several cuttings from one long shoot, cutting just above a leaf at the top and just below at the base. They will take the whole winter to root, but be patient: the worst thing you can do is keep pulling them up for a look (you will break any new roots as they form).

Lavender is easily propagated by taking semi-ripe cuttings in summer.

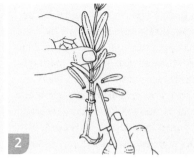

1 Select a shoot from a healthy plant, ideally about 8cm (3in) long, with about 1cm (½in) of brown, woody stem at the base. If it is a sideshoot, pull it away from the plant (with a short 'heel' of main stem) and if it is a shoot-tip cutting, cut it away about 8cm (3in) below the shoot.

2 Using a sharp garden knife, remove the lower leaves from the lower two-thirds of the stem, as well as any thorns from prickly plants. Pinch out any sappy shoot tips. Trim the heel to remove any long whiskers. The prepared cuttings should be about 10cm (4in) long.

3 For plants that need help in order to root, such as clematis, dip the cut end into a saucer filled with hormone rooting powder and tap off the surplus. Push the cuttings around the edge of a pot filled with damp seed and cutting compost or multipurpose compost.

4 Cover the pot with a clear plastic bag, held in place with an elastic band. While the plants are rooting, stand the pot in a well-lit spot, but out of direct sunlight. Check the cuttings after two or three weeks and once they have rooted, pot them up separately.

Hormone rooting preparations

With some plant cuttings, such as those of clematis, it can be extremely difficult to get them to root without a little extra help from a hormone rooting powder or gel. Others, such as pelargoniums, do not need it – in fact, it will make the stem rot. If you can't find out whether to use it for a particular plant, you can always hedge your bets by planting up two pots of cuttings – one treated with rooting preparation, one untreated. Bear in mind that hormone rooting powders and gels have a limited life, which will be shortened further if they become contaminated. Tip out only a small amount into a saucer for immediate use and close the container again. When you have finished, throw away any powder remaining in the saucer, rather than tipping it back into the container.

Taking hardwood cuttings is an ideal propagation method for deciduous shrubs with long, straight stems such as roses, dogwoods (*Cornus*), willows (*Salix*), hazel (*Corylus*) and vines (*Vitis*). Some plants, for instance dogwoods, willows, forsythias and philadelphus, root more easily than others and can be inserted direct into the garden soil or into a pot of compost to root. Others need a hormone rooting preparation as well as compost.

Division

This is one of the simplest ways to propagate plants. Digging up and dividing old perennials is a good means of splitting large clumps of plants where the centre of the plant often dies off. This method is suited to plants that have spreading root systems or produce new growth from the base, such as hostas, daylilies (*Hemerocallis*) and some primulas. It allows you to keep the healthier outer parts, discard the old pieces and multiply your stock. As you replant, you can give the new pieces of plant more space and fresh compost to keep them growing and healthy. Most perennials should be divided between late autumn and early spring, but not during extreme weather conditions.

You can also use division to multiply your bulbs, such as irises, lilies (*Lilium*), tulips (*Tulipa*), daffodils (*Narcissus*), snowdrops (*Galanthus*) and hyacinths (*Hyacinthus*), and improve flowering. Simply lift and divide the bulbs if they're overcrowded, splitting 'daughter' bulbs away from the parent, and replanting in another container.

HOW TO propagate hardwood cuttings

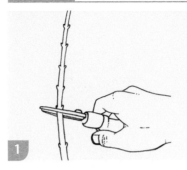

1 Using secateurs, remove a length of healthy stem from the current year's growth. Make a straight cut. If there are sideshoots present, trim them off.

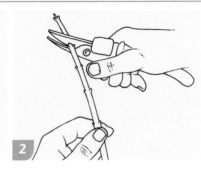

2 Trim the top of the shoot, making a sloping cut just above a bud. The cutting should be about 20cm (8in) long. You may need to dip the base in hormone rooting powder.

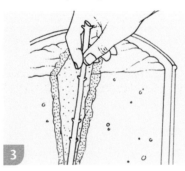

3 Fill a pot with free-draining cutting compost and moisten the compost well. Make a small slit trench in the compost. Insert the cutting into the trench, base first, leaving only the top third of the cutting showing above the surface.

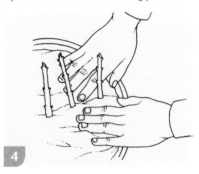

4 Continue inserting cuttings, then close the trench by firming compost around it. Water well and stand the pot in a well-lit, frost-free, sheltered spot outside over winter. Once the cuttings have rooted, pot them up separately.

Root and leaf cuttings

Root cuttings are an unusual means of propagation that works for plants that do not respond well to division, for example the alpine types of phlox, campsis, wisteria and *Anemone × hybrida*. It can be done while plants are dormant, between winter and early spring. Dig up an established plant and wash the roots in a bucket of water. Select a young, fleshy root and cut it into sections with a clean, sharp knife, making a straight cut at the top and a slanted cut at the base. Pull off any fibrous side roots. Roots of around a pencil's thickness can be pushed vertically into pots of John Innes No. 1 or multipurpose compost so that the tip is just buried. Thinner roots can be laid horizontally in trays of compost. Once you see new shoots emerging, pot up the plants individually.

Leaf cuttings are a way of propagating plants that don't have any stems, such as African violets (*Saintpaulia*), *Begonia rex* and many succulents. Root African violet leaves complete with their leaf-stalks individually. Cut a healthy leaf from *Begonia rex*, slice it up into sections, about 3cm (1½in) square, remembering which is the top and bottom of the leaf. Insert the cuttings into seed compost, burying the bottom 1cm (½in) of the leaf section and leaving the rest sticking out. Keep the cuttings in a warm propagator. When a young plant has been produced at the bottom of each of them, pot them up individually.

HOW TO divide clump-forming perennials

1 Using a trowel, work your way around the sides of the pot containing the perennials to be divided (here, hostas). Tip the pot upside down to release the rootball.

2 Where the roots divide naturally, dig through the clump with a sharp spade to divide it in two. Repeat if required to produce more, smaller clumps.

3 Plant the smaller clumps immediately into new containers filled with compost. Don't delay or the plants may dry out. Water thoroughly after planting.

Which propagation method?

	BEST PROPAGATION METHOD	SEASON
BULBS, CORMS AND RHIZOMES	Division	Late autumn to early spring
ANNUALS AND BIENNIALS	Seed	Depends on flowering times and temperatures needed for germination
PERENNIALS		
Perennials with spreading root systems and producing lots of shoots from the base *Achillea, Aster, Astrantia, Helianthus, Hemerocallis, Heuchera, Hosta, Lychnis, Ophiopogon, Phormium, Primula, Sedum, Veronica*	Division	Late autumn to early spring
Bushy herbaceous perennials that root quickly and have long stems *Argyranthemum, Diascia, Gazania, Impatiens, Osteospermum, Pelargonium, Penstemon, Solenostemon*	Softwood cuttings	Spring or summer
TREES, SHRUBS AND ROSES		
Shrubs that root easily *Fuchsia, Helichrysum petiolare, Hydrangea, Viburnum*	Softwood cuttings	Spring or summer
Conifers, many evergreen shrubs and some deciduous shrubs *Aucuba, Berberis, Buxus, Callistemon, Calluna, Camellia, Ceanothus, Choisya, Cistus, Cotoneaster, Cytisus, Elaeagnus, Erica, Garrya, Griselinia, Hebe, Ilex, Lavandula, Magnolia grandiflora, Mahonia, Olearia, Pieris, Prunus (evergreen), Rhododendron, Rosmarinus, Skimmia, Weigela*	Semi-ripe cuttings	Mid- to late summer
Deciduous shrubs with long, straight stems *Cornus, Corylus, Forsythia, Philadelphus, Rosa, Salix, Vitis*	Hardwood cuttings	Mid-autumn to early spring

Plants for containers

There are countless plants that will grow well in containers, not just bedding and bulbs but trees, shrubs, climbers, and even edible crops. There is a plant for every season, wherever you live, so you need never have a barren container garden, even in winter. When buying plants, don't restrict yourself to the local garden centre, which may stock only a limited range; browse through seed and plant catalogues and gardening websites to see what's on offer. Visit open gardens and historic properties for ideas and to see what the plants you want to grow actually look like as they get bigger.

Trees and shrubs

Trees and shrubs grow very happily in containers. They provide height and structure, and will reward you with their attractive flowers, leaves, bark or stems. You do need to bear in mind the fact that they're long-lived and often quite large plants that have a high requirement for both water and food if they're to thrive. They also need quite a bit of space. Containers for these larger plants need to be roomy and stable, because the increased height makes it more likely that a strong wind will blow them over. Select a pot with a wide base and vertical, rather than angled, sides. It needs to be deep enough to accommodate a stake, if necessary, and should be as water-retentive as possible. This section has been divided into deciduous and evergreen plants – the former tend to be more striking at certain times of the year, while the latter provide the structural framework for permanent, year-round displays.

KEY to symbols used

In this chapter the following symbols are used to indicate a plant's preferred growing conditions. Unless otherwise specified, plants are fully hardy. Those in a blue-tinted box are particularly recommended for their reliability.

○ Prefers/tolerates an open, sunny site
◑ Prefers/tolerates some shade
● Prefers/tolerates full shade
✹ Will survive winter in a sheltered site
❀ Always needs protection from frost
pH↓ Needs ericaceous compost
❖ Season of main interest (e.g. for flowers, foliage, stems, berries)

Deciduous trees and shrubs

Deciduous plants (those that lose their leaves in autumn) are a vital addition to any container display. Many of them produce attractive flowers, and a high percentage of them also have a second season of interest in autumn as the leaves change colour. Where space for growing is limited, this can be an important factor in your selection, as every plant you introduce really has to earn its place.

Some deciduous trees and shrubs have attractive bark, or interesting stems and branches that add another dimension in winter. These are especially good value in containers. However, if you have your heart set on a plant that looks wonderful in summer but seems to lose its magic when it loses its leaves, you needn't avoid it altogether: underplanting it with spring bulbs and/or low-growing evergreen perennials will compensate for its temporary shortcomings.

Acer Maple
○ ◑ ❖ SPRING, AUTUMN

The Japanese maples are *A. japonicum* and *A. palmatum*. Both are deciduous and include a range of beautifully coloured and highly decorative shrubs and trees. The season of interest is long, ranging from brightly coloured new growth in spring to fiery autumn tints, and the leaves may be entire or so dissected that they are fern-like. These are unrivalled as architectural specimen plants, set in individual containers where they can be viewed from all sides. They will grow better with protection from cold winds, which can 'burn' the delicate foliage, and golden forms need shade from intense sun, which can scorch them.

Albizia julibrissin Silk tree
○ ✹ ❖ SUMMER

A large shrub or small tree with attractive, fern-like foliage, the silk tree bears clusters of fluffy-looking, spherical, lime-green flowers. The form *A.j.* f. *rosea* has pretty, candy-pink blooms. This plant begins to produce flowers after only a few years, and makes a beautiful specimen tree. It is a good choice for a sunny, sheltered patio or terrace, or a courtyard, where there is enough warmth for the plant to flower well. If you need to move it into a conservatory over the winter, make sure you choose a pot that is light enough to move around.

Amelanchier lamarckii
Snowy mespilus
○ ◑ pH ❖ SPRING, AUTUMN

This is an upright shrub that may be allowed to grow into a small tree. It prefers ericaceous compost and can tolerate pollution. The new shoots are covered in silky-white hairs and the leaves are bronze-green. In autumn, they turn fiery orange and red. The star-like, white flowers make a wonderful display in spring. In summer, this plant may fade into the background, but you can liven it up by growing a smaller clematis through the branches.

Betula utilis var. jacquemontii
Silver birch
○ ◑ ❖ SPRING, AUTUMN

The silver birch is grown for its white stem and delicate canopy, which provides lovely dappled shade. It would eventually become a large, conical tree but its growth is restricted in a container. Catkins are borne on the tree in spring and the leaves turn buttery yellow in autumn before they fall. Some birches have whiter stems than others, so have a look at several before you buy.

Buddleja davidii Butterfly bush
○ ❖ SUMMER

The butterfly bush is an excellent beginner's plant that not only provides wonderful spikes of highly fragrant, white, pink, blue or purple (as in 'Black Knight', above) flowers, but attracts butterflies and bees too. It is tolerant of exposure, pollution and some neglect, and grows tall enough to make a good screen. For the best flowers, prune it hard every spring. Stand it behind other plants and allow it lots of room to grow.

Caragana arborescens Pea tree
○ ❖ LATE SPRING

The pea tree is an erect, thorny large shrub or small tree with light-green leaves and pretty, pale-yellow flowers in late spring, followed by brown seedpods in autumn. Do not allow it to become waterlogged. It tolerates poor, dry soils in cold and exposed positions. The pea tree is a great plant for a windy site and is also available as a grafted standard ('Pendula'), which makes an ideal single-specimen tree when used as a focal point in a large pot in the garden.

Chaenomeles speciosa
Flowering quince
○ ◑ ❖ EARLY to MID-SPRING

This spiny, pollution-tolerant shrub is grown for its cheery, cup-shaped flowers, followed by edible, apple-like fruit in autumn (the warmer the position, the better the fruit). It can get a bit tangled if neglected, but is lovely trained against a wall; add interest by growing a smaller form of summer- or autumn-flowering clematis through it. There are several varieties, with single or double flowers in reds, pinks and white.

Cornus kousa Chinese dogwood
○ ◑ ❖ SUMMER, AUTUMN

There are several forms of this small, broadly conical tree. All have flaking bark, wavy-edged leaves that turn crimson in autumn and green flowers in early summer, sometimes followed by inedible, strawberry-like red fruits. Flowers are tiny but are surrounded by showy, white or pink bracts that resemble big flowers. This is a lovely tree worth seeking out, especially the smaller forms, such as 'Satomi' (above) or the gold-variegated 'Gold Star'.

Corylus avellana 'Contorta'
Contorted hazel
◯ ◑ ❖ WINTER to SPRING

With its corkscrew-like stems, the contorted hazel makes a fascinating specimen plant. It produces long, golden catkins in spring along with small, insignificant red flowers. The twisted stems look particularly good in winter and are super in indoor arrangements. Keep it in shape by regular pruning.

Cytisus battandieri
Pineapple broom
◯ ❄ ❖ SUMMER

The pineapple broom is a small, upright tree or large shrub grown for its golden yellow flowers. It has a delicious pineapple fragrance, scenting the air on a warm, calm day. The new leaves are covered with fine, silky hairs, giving them a silvery sheen. This plant can be trained to grow as a wall shrub on a south-facing wall, but it does not recover from hard pruning into older wood. It is a good, tall plant for the back of a display, where the foliage sets off the smaller plants in front.

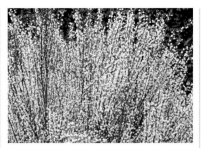

Cytisus × praecox Broom
◯ ❖ SPRING

This compact deciduous shrub forms a mound of arching shoots with tiny green leaves and cream flowers (above, 'Albus'). It can tolerate exposure to wind and is useful for exposed coastal areas. It is a distinctive plant that is best in a pot or container on its own, although you could add early-flowering bulbs for colour while it is still dormant.

Forsythia × intermedia
◯ ◑ ❖ SPRING

This forsythia is one of the earliest deciduous shrubs to flower in spring and one of the easiest for the beginner. Regular pruning keeps it under control and ensures a plentiful supply of glorious yellow, four-petalled flowers (above, 'Lynwood'). Some forms are more compact than others. Lush green foliage provides a summer backdrop to other plants. Forsythias are tolerant of pollution so are good for urban areas. Look out for a variegated form for added summer interest.

Fuchsia
◯ ◑ ▦ (some species) ❖ SUMMER to AUTUMN

This is a large group of deciduous and evergreen shrubs, grown for their attractive flowers and/or foliage (above, 'Alan Titchmarsh'). They flower profusely in summer and autumn, and there is a fuchsia for every situation within the container garden, from a large standard to a tiny pot; trailing varieties will fill a hanging basket. The flowers are classified as single, semi-double, double or tubular. Most are not fully hardy, but you can overwinter the plants (or any cuttings from them) ready for next year.

Hydrangea macrophylla
Common hydrangea
◯ ◑ pH↓ (for blue) ❖ SUMMER to AUTUMN

The common hydrangea is a rounded shrub with cultivars divided into two groups: Hortensias and Lacecaps, according to the shape of the flower-head. Hortensias have large, mophead blooms (as above) and Lacecaps have flattened clusters of flowers. Flower colour is influenced by soil acidity; blue hydrangeas need to be kept in ericaceous compost, or they will change to pink or red.

Lagerstroemia indica
Crepe flower
○ ✿ ❖ MIDSUMMER to AUTUMN

The crepe flower develops into an upright large shrub or small tree with peeling, grey-brown bark. The dark-green leaves are delicately tinted bronze as they emerge, but it is grown mainly for the dense clusters of small flowers in colours from pure white through pink to red, lavender and purple. This plant loves a hot spot, such as a sunny patio, but bring it under cover in winter.

Leycesteria formosa
Himalayan nutmeg
○ ◑ ❖ SUMMER to EARLY AUTUMN

This easy, spreading shrub forms a good windbreak in a container. It has tall, bamboo-like green shoots and thick foliage. The flowers are white with red bracts and hang in clusters. The bracts remain around the purplish-red berries that form as the flowers fade. The green stems are attractive in winter and thick enough to provide screening all year.

Philadelphus microphyllus
Mock orange
○ ◑ ❖ LATE SPRING to MIDSUMMER

This mock orange is a highly fragrant shrub, producing masses of beautiful white, single blooms in summer, with a heavy scent of orange blossom. It has chestnut-brown, peeling bark that can be seen in winter once the leaves have fallen. This philadelphus is smaller than most of the others, at around 1m (3ft), but you can plant several and trim them to form a low screen. It is tolerant of pollution.

Prunus Ornamental cherry
○ ◑ ❖ SPRING/AUTUMN to SPRING

Ornamental cherries are grown for their attractive single, semi-double or double flowers in white, pink or red as well as their superb range of autumn colours and ornamental bark. They flower better if the roots are slightly restricted in the container. *P.* × *subhirtella* 'Autumnalis' (above) is a small, spreading tree that flowers periodically in late autumn, winter and early spring when mild. *P. tenella* 'Fire Hill' is a bushy shrub with glossy, dark-green foliage and dark-pink flowers. (*See also* box, opposite.)

Rosa rugosa Hedgehog rose, Japanese rose, Ramanas rose
○ ❖ SUMMER

This is a versatile, tolerant shrub rose with dense, very prickly stems. It has wrinkled, rough leaves and highly fragrant single or semi-double flowers, depending on the form. The flowers are often followed by plump, tomato-like hips, which last well into winter. This is an attractive and useful boundary plant able to withstand pollution and wind. In a mixed planting, stand it among other plants so there is no danger of scratching yourself on the stems.

Sambucus nigra 'Eva' Elder
○ ❖ SPRING

This form of elder has the most glorious dark, dissected (almost ferny) foliage that is attractive even without the flattened clusters of delicate, pale-pink flowers in spring. This is a large deciduous shrub that really needs a container to itself and will work well in a black or monochrome planting scheme as well as providing a stunning backdrop for other plants in a mixed display.

Viburnum × bodnantense 'Dawn'

○ ◐ ❖WINTER

This upright shrub gives a particularly wonderful display in winter, with clusters of heavily fragrant white, pink-budded flowers on bare stems. In a good year, it flowers from late autumn to spring. Make sure you can reach it in winter to smell the fantastic fragrance.

Weigela florida

○ ◐ ❖SUMMER

This is a really easy beginner's plant that will grow in any position except deep shade. Masses of tubular red or pink flowers are produced all over the plant in early summer. Trim it annually after flowering to keep it under control.

Other ornamental cherry trees for containers

Prunus 'Fudan-zakura'
○ ❖AUTUMN to SPRING
Clusters of pink buds open to single white flowers from autumn to spring. Coppery young leaves.

Prunus 'Pandora'
○ ❖SPRING, AUTUMN
Masses of pale-pink flowers in early spring. Good autumn foliage.

Prunus 'Spire'
○ ❖SPRING, AUTUMN
Pale-pink flower clusters in spring and colourful leaves in autumn.

Evergreen trees and shrubs

Evergreen plants don't have two separate seasons of foliage interest in the same way as some deciduous ones, but they offer the chance to develop a backbone or framework in the design. This will remain in place throughout the year and the other, more transient, plantings can be woven around it. Conifers have been out of fashion for a while, but they have a valuable contribution to make to the year-round structure of a design, especially in the container garden, where seasonal variety is particularly important. Seek out very small, slow-growing conifers.

Acacia dealbata Mimosa, Wattle

○ ❄ ❖WINTER to SPRING

Wattle has delicate foliage and, sometimes, quite vicious thorns that are a useful deterrent to trespassers. Fluffy yellow flowers are produced in late winter and early spring and are usually sweetly fragrant. It resents hard pruning, so prune little and often to maintain the shape. Most varieties can be trained against a sunny wall. There are both evergreen and deciduous types. Acacias prefer a warm, sheltered, sunny corner, so are ideal for a hot patio, terrace or courtyard. They look particularly good in ceramic or terracotta containers to complete the feeling of being in a warmer country.

Aucuba japonica Spotted laurel

◐ ● ❖YEAR-ROUND

The spotted laurel is an attractive shrub with large, glossy leaves and big berries. It is very tolerant and will grow almost anywhere, even in shade, polluted areas and by the coast. Small, purple-red flowers appear in spring, followed (on female plants, such as 'Crotonifolia', above) by bright red berries that last into winter. This is the plant to try when all else has failed. Just keep it in a water-retentive pot (for example plastic or plastic-lined wood) to ensure it has enough moisture around the roots.

Berberis darwinii Barberry

○ ◐ ❖SPRING, AUTUMN

This is a dense plant, with spiny, dark-green leaves like a miniature holly. It produces a glorious display of orange flowers in spring and often again in autumn, followed by blue-black berries. It responds well to regular trimming and makes a good boundary plant to deter trespassers. It is also pollution-tolerant, so will grow well in the town or city.

Buxus sempervirens Box
○ ◐ ❖SPRING

Box is a hardy, slow-growing, bushy plant that makes a good foil to brightly coloured plants or can be clipped to form topiary shapes. It has small, glossy green leaves and masses of tiny, star-shaped, yellowish-green flowers in spring. It is tolerant of hard pruning, but prefers to be trimmed little and often. If you are using it as topiary, choose a pot that will complement the shape and where you intend to place it; you can be as formal or informal as you like.

Callistemon citrinus
Crimson bottlebrush
○ ❄ pH↓ ❖SPRING to SUMMER

This exotic-looking Australian plant has silky, pink-tinted young shoots and leathery leaves. Bottlebrush-like clusters of flowers in shades of red (above, 'Splendens'), pink, purple, white, yellow or green are produced at the tips of shoots, although the growth then continues beyond them. This is another plant that needs a hot spot such as a sunny patio or deck or a warm, sheltered courtyard if it is to flower well.

Camellia
◐ ◑ ● (some species) pH↓ ❖SPRING to SUMMER

Camellias are lovely shrubs with glossy foliage and spectacular flowers in white, cream, pink or red (above, 'Spring Festival'). Blooms are single, semi-double, double, anemone-form, peony-form or rose-form. Camellias are ideal for containers, but need ericaceous compost and a constant supply of water, as drought causes the buds to be shed unopened. Make sure your camellia has plenty of room to grow in its pot and feed it regularly.

Ceanothus California lilac
○ ❖LATE SPRING to MIDSUMMER

Most forms of ceanothus dislike cold winds, so are best planted in a sheltered position against a wall in a large, sturdy container so they can grow well. 'Blue Mound' (above) is a dense, bushy shrub flowering in late spring to early summer. *C. dentatus*, producing dark-blue flowers in fluffy-looking spikes in late spring, is more spreading but responds well to light pruning to keep it in shape.

Chamaecyparis lawsoniana
Lawson cypress
○ ◐ ❖YEAR-ROUND

This attractive, densely leafy conifer and its cultivars grow slowly to form architectural shapes, giving year-round structure. Trim as necessary, but do not cut into old wood, because it will not regrow. There are several shapes and colours available that will not outgrow a container too quickly, including the dwarf, rounded 'Gnome', with blue-green foliage, and 'Minima glauca' (above, in frost), with sea-green leaves.

Choisya ternata
Mexican orange blossom
○ ❖LATE SPRING, LATE SUMMER to AUTUMN

This is an attractive, tolerant shrub with glossy, aromatic leaves. Dense clusters of fragrant white, star-shaped flowers are produced in late spring and in late summer and autumn. 'Sundance' has bright-yellow foliage. *C.* × *dewitteana* 'Aztec Pearl' is relatively compact, with long, thin, dark-green leaves.

Clianthus puniceus Lobster claw
○ ❄ ❖ SPRING to SUMMER

This is an evergreen shrub with shoots that will climb or trail. From spring to summer, bright-red flowers, which are shaped like lobster claws and hang in clusters, peep out from between dark-green leaves. White and pink forms are also available, but they are slightly less exotic-looking than the red. This plant is ideal in a sheltered, warm courtyard or similar spot, especially where you want to create a tropical effect.

Cryptomeria japonica 'Elegans Compacta' Japanese cedar
○ ◑ ❖ SPRING, WINTER

This Japanese cedar is an unusual, conical conifer with soft, glossy, dark-green foliage that turns a burnished bronze in winter. It has thick, fibrous, red-brown bark and produces small, round cones. This is one conifer that responds well to clipping and can be shaped to fit in with a Japanese design, where it can look very impressive as a specimen plant in a plain-coloured container.

Erica carnea Heath
○ pH ❖ YEAR-ROUND (if cultivars are selected)

Heaths are low-growing shrubs that prefer acid growing conditions, so they combine well with heathers, pieris and rhododendrons. Many have bronze or golden foliage that is attractive even without the small, bell-shaped flowers of white, pink (above, 'Springwood Pink'), red or mauve. Heaths have similar-looking foliage to some conifers, and they complement each other when combined in a container display.

Cotoneaster cashmiriensis
○ ◑ ❖ SUMMER, AUTUMN

This is an attractive shrub with glossy foliage, small, creamy-white flowers (pink in bud) and showy, bright-red berries. Its prostrate habit makes it ideal for using in containers or troughs, where it can weep forwards, covering the pot in a green curtain. This cotoneaster grows well among other plants, where it acts as a living mulch. The flowers and berries give a long period of interest. It is tolerant of pollution, so is good in urban areas.

Elaeagnus × ebbingei
○ ❖ AUTUMN to EARLY WINTER

This reliable, hardy shrub is suitable for any situation and is ideal for making a screen or windbreak. It has small, white, bell-like flowers that are highly fragrant but, because they are produced beneath the leaves, you often notice the scent before you spot them. The shoots and sea-green leaves have an attractive, scaly, bronze sheen that glows in sunlight. They are tolerant of pollution, so would make a good screen on a town balcony.

Escallonia
○ ❖ SUMMER

Versatile shrubs with a lovely range of flower colours from white ('Iveyi') through pink ('Apple Blossom', above) to scarlet ('Langleyensis'). The flowers are produced in clusters amid glossy, dark-green leaves. This plant responds well to regular light pruning and is useful as a wall shrub and for providing shelter in coastal areas, as it can tolerate salty winds.

Euonymus fortunei
○ ◐ ❖YEAR-ROUND

This low-growing shrub and its cultivars (above, 'Emerald 'n' Gold') have spectacularly colourful foliage, which often flushes pink in winter, and insignificant greenish-white flowers. They can be treated as scrambling climbers if given some support, or the stems can be left to trail. They can grow almost anywhere and thrive in full sun and poor soil.

Garrya elliptica 'James Roof'
Silk-tassel bush
○ ◐ ❖WINTER

This is a magnificent plant for winter interest. The leaves are a dark sea green on long, upright stems. In winter, it produces long, silvery-grey, tassel-like catkins that gradually lengthen and open to reveal golden anthers. The catkins last many weeks and move in the slightest breeze. It is hardy enough to grow as a windbreak in a coastal area.

Griselinia littoralis Broadleaf
○ ◐ ❖YEAR-ROUND

Most gardeners grow this dense, upright shrub for its handsome, rounded, apple-green foliage, but it is very tolerant of wind (even salt-laden coastal winds) and is useful as a windbreak. Yellow-green male and female flowers are borne on separate plants, so both are needed to produce the purple fruits. This is a good choice where you want a larger shrub, as it will fill whatever container you put it in.

Fatsia japonica False castor oil
◐ ● ❖SPRING

The large, leathery leaves of this handsome, wide-spreading evergreen make this an impressive specimen plant and a great addition to a tropical theme or where you need a focal point in shade. As the plant matures, it produces creamy-white flowers. It grows quickly and needs plenty of room, but large plants can be pruned hard in spring to remove up to half the growth. The shape of the plant is better if it is given space, as it can become leggy if it is crowded in with other plants.

Gaultheria mucronata (syn. Pernettya mucronata)
○ pH↓ ❖SUMMER, WINTER

This is a compact, bushy shrub that prefers a shady position and acid conditions. It has leathery leaves and bell-shaped white flowers, followed by pretty, round berries of white, pink, red or purple. Male and female plants must be grown together for fruit to form. This is a good plant for winter interest and combines well with other acid-lovers like heathers (Calluna), heaths (Erica), pieris and rhododendrons.

Hebe Shrubby veronica
○ ◐ ❄ (some species) ❖SUMMER to AUTUMN

Hebes are low-growing shrubs that are valued for their attractive foliage and long period of flowering. Small flowers are borne in large, densely packed clusters, in colours ranging from white to blue, red and pink (as in 'Watson's Pink', above). They are ideal plants for containers, tolerating some pollution and thriving in mild areas, particularly near the coast. They range in size from very small (H. cupressoides 'Boughton Dome') to large shrubs (H. 'Great Orme' and H. 'Marjorie').

Helichrysum italicum
○ ❄ ❖ SUMMER, AUTUMN

This is a bushy sub-shrub with narrow, aromatic, curry-scented, silver leaves and small, yellow, daisy-like flowers in summer and autumn. Like most silver-leaved plants, it is good in a hot area, prefers slightly dry compost and will tolerate wind as long as it's not really cold. It needs protection from excessive winter wet and frosts. It looks good with herbs and works well in a mixed display.

Lantana camara
○ ❖ SUMMER

A small, variable shrub with coarsely textured leaves and bristly stems that burst into colour as the flowers open. These may be white, yellow, orange, pink or red and change colour as they age, so that as the cluster opens from the outside towards the centre, there will be individual flowers in a range of shades, giving a spectacular effect. This heat-lover is good for a sunny patio, balcony or terrace, but it will need winter protection from low temperatures.

Magnolia grandiflora
○ ◑ ❖ MID- to LATE SUMMER

This magnolia grows to form a large shrub, and responds well to being trained against a wall. It has glossy leaves that give cover all year round and cup-shaped white flowers. The form 'Little Gem' (above) is fairly compact and is well suited to growing in a container. It has dark-green leaves that are rusty-brown underneath.

Kalmia latifolia Calico bush
○ ◑ pH ❖ LATE SPRING to MIDSUMMER

The calico bush is a dense evergreen shrub with glossy, dark-green leaves. From late spring until midsummer, it produces large clusters of extremely pretty, bowl-shaped, pink or white flowers. Pinch out the shoot tips regularly to encourage bushiness, but do not hard prune because it will take years to recover. This is a good plant for a semi-shaded area as it is a woodlander that prefers moist, acid soil and it will thrive if you plant it in ericaceous compost.

Lavandula Lavender
○ ❄ (some species) ❖ SUMMER

Lavenders are grown mainly for their aromatic purple, blue, pink or white flowers carried in narrow spikes on long, tough stems. Their silvery-green leaves are covered with fine hairs that are effective at preventing moisture loss. French lavender (L. stoechas) has a tuft on top of the flower spike and prefers slightly acidic compost. All lavenders enjoy a hot position with shelter from cold winds. They are wonderful plants for a seating area, as the sun releases the volatile oils.

Myrtus communis Myrtle
○ ❖ SUMMER, AUTUMN

Myrtle is a pretty, upright, bushy shrub with small, aromatic leaves and it will thrive in the shelter of a warm wall. The small, fragrant, creamy-white flowers have prominent stamens forming a fluffy-looking central tuft and are followed by black fruit. It responds to light trimming, so you can shape the plant, like informal topiary. The leaves are also aromatic and release their fragrance in the heat of the sun, so it is a good plant to have near your seating area, where you can appreciate the scent.

Nandina domestica 'Fire Power'
Heavenly bamboo
○ ❄ ❖SUMMER

This low evergreen or semi-evergreen shrub resembles a bamboo but is actually related to *Berberis*. It is a striking plant with upright shoots and bright-red foliage that is particularly colourful after a frost. The small, white, star-shaped flowers are produced in upright clusters. This is a good plant to have near a doorway or seating area, where you can hear the breeze rustling the leaves.

Olea europaea Olive
○ ❄ ❖SUMMER

The olive is a slow-growing shrub or small tree with leathery grey-green leaves. It has tiny, fragrant white flowers in summer, followed by oval, green fruit that may ripen to black. Olives are becoming very popular in gardens, but not all will survive a cold winter and some protection is wise. They are attractive, architectural plants that are ideal for adding to a Mediterranean design in a large ceramic or terracotta container.

Osmanthus × burkwoodii
◑ ❖SPRING

This is a dense, rounded shrub with leathery, dark-green leaves. It responds well to clipping and can be trained as topiary or a screen, or against a wall; it is particularly useful for a town garden, as it is tolerant of pollution. The white flowers are very fragrant, tubular in shape and produced in clusters.

Picea mariana 'Nana'
Black spruce
○ ◑ ❖SPRING

This pretty little conifer grows slowly into a rounded shape with short, densely packed branches. The leaves are blue-grey with a whitish stripe underneath. As it grows only about 3cm (1½in) a year, it is ideal for a container, where it will mix well with small alpine plants or heathers, giving colour and interest all year round.

Pieris japonica
○ ◑ pH↓ ❖SPRING

This upright to rounded shrub is spectacular in spring, when the new bright-red shoots emerge at the same time as masses of small, white or pink, bell-shaped flowers, depending on the variety (above: 'White Rim', left; 'Carnaval', right). It prefers ericaceous compost and shelter from cold winds and frost and looks good in a display of acid-loving plants, together with heathers (*Calluna*) and rhododendrons.

Rhododendron
○ ◑ ● pH↓ ❖SPRING to SUMMER

Rhododendrons consist of both evergreen and deciduous shrubs, although the deciduous ones are often classified as azaleas. The evergreens have bell-shaped flowers in purples, reds, pinks (as in 'Cilpinense', above), pale yellow and white, amid bold green foliage. Some have leaves with a fuzzy brown covering of hairs or scales on the undersides. All rhododendrons need ericaceous compost and do best in partial shade. Dead-head after flowering to stop seed forming.

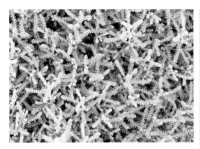

Santolina chamaecyparissus
Cotton lavender
○ ❖SUMMER

Cotton lavender is a dense, rounded shrub with aromatic, greyish-white foliage and woolly, white young shoots. In summer it is covered with small yellow flowers. This is a good shrub for a hot, sunny area and it will tolerate being slightly dry. It will also cope with wind and is useful at the coast, although it dislikes winter wet and cold winds.

Sarcococca confusa
Christmas box
○ ◑ ● ❖WINTER

This is a tolerant, elegant, low-growing shrub that can cope with pollution, shade and limited neglect, but dislikes cold winds, making it a good choice for a sheltered but shady courtyard. The flowers, which are produced abundantly over winter and are followed by black berries, release an amazing fragrance on a calm day. This shrub responds well to light but regular trimming.

Skimmia japonica
○ ◑ ● ❖WINTER to SPRING

Tolerant of atmospheric pollution, this low-growing aromatic shrub is ideal for inner city use and a sheltered, shady courtyard. Small, fragrant flowers open from reddish buds, followed by long-lasting, crimson berries on female plants. For berries, you need both male (as in 'Rubella', above) and female plants.

Taxus baccata 'Standishii' Yew
○ ❖SPRING

This female form of the common yew has golden foliage and grows into a narrow, columnar shape. It has scaly, rich-brown bark and, like other forms of yew, tolerates pollution and exposure. It may have fleshy, red, poisonous fruits in autumn. Yew responds well to clipping and is one of the few conifers that will regrow from old wood. This is a good alternative if you do not have room for a tree, but give it gritty, well-drained soil in a decent-sized container.

Thuja occidentalis White cedar
○ ❖YEAR-ROUND

The white cedar may not change much throughout the year, but it does add a welcome splash of colour in winter. Its rounded, conical shape is also an attractive feature. There are several cultivars: 'Rheingold' is a striking golden-orange colour and, if crushed, the foliage smells of crystallized oranges; 'Caespitosa' is slow-growing, green and cushion-shaped with slightly ferny-looking foliage; 'Europa Gold' (above) has golden foliage. Underplant with small, spring-flowering bulbs.

Trachycarpus fortunei
Chusan palm
○ ◑ ❖LATE SPRING to EARLY SUMMER

This is a tall, upright palm with very big, fan-shaped leaves. It grows slowly, developing a single, furry trunk made up of fibrous remains of old leaf-stalks. Small yellow flowers appear in large, dense bunches up to 60cm (24in) long; in a very hot summer, the flowers may be followed by black, date-like fruits, 1cm (½in) across. Plant anywhere you need a tropical effect. It grows best with some shelter.

Climbers

Climbing plants are a great way to add height to your display. Whether you grow them up an obelisk, train them on trellis or a wall, or let them trail over a balcony railing, they will provide welcome colour, cover and interest for much of the year. Climbers are particularly useful where space is limited: if you make use of vertical spaces, such as a flat wall, you can fit more plants into the area. A wall covered in attractive greenery also helps to create a feeling of enclosure and privacy.

Humulus lupulus 'Aureus'
Golden hop
○ ◑ ❖ SPRING, SUMMER

The golden hop is a self-supporting, herbaceous perennial climber with thin, bristly, twining stems. In summer, insignificant green flowers are produced, followed in autumn by clusters of fruit (hops). It can even thrive in a north-facing site, although the spring growth may be a little delayed. The dried stems and flowers can be used for indoor arrangements.

Eccremocarpus scaber
Chilean glory flower
○ ❄ ❖ SUMMER to AUTUMN

This is an unusual perennial, evergreen climber that can be quite fast-growing in the right place. Often treated as an annual because of its inability to cope with low temperatures, it likes a warm position. It needs a deep pot and loam-based compost to grow well.

Akebia quinata Chocolate vine
○ ◑ ❖ SPRING

Known as the chocolate vine, this semi-evergreen twining climber is grown for its bronze-tinted young leaves and attractive, rich maroon to chocolate-brown, vanilla-scented flowers in spring. The long, purple, sausage-shaped fruits are produced only if there is a second plant near by to pollinate. To fruit well, it needs a warm spring and long, hot summer. Akebia looks good when grown densely on a pergola in an attractive container.

Hedera Ivy
○ ◑ ❖ AUTUMN

Ivies are evergreen, self-clinging climbers with aerial roots that attach themselves to almost any surface. Many cultivars have attractive variegation. Small-leaved varieties such as *H. helix* cultivars will trail downwards as well as climb. Large-leaved forms such as *H. colchica* 'Dentata Variegata' (above) are ideal for covering a wall or fence, and need a good-sized pot.

Ipomoea lobata Spanish flag
○ ❋ ❖ SUMMER to AUTUMN

A perennial climber, this morning glory is usually treated as an annual. It has red stems and leaf-stalks with green leaves. The flowers are produced in dense, one-sided spikes and open red, maturing to orange and yellow, so there can be all three colours on the spike at once. The hot-coloured flowers blend well with a hot or tropical display.

Jasminum nudiflorum
Winter jasmine
○ ◑ ❖ WINTER

Winter jasmine is a shrubby, sprawling plant that can be trained against a wall, trellis or fence. It produces masses of yellow flowers (which are ideal for indoor arrangements) throughout winter and early spring. It needs trimming regularly or it gets quite tatty. The form 'Aureum' has yellow-marked leaves. Grow this long-lived plant in a large container, such as a wooden half-barrel.

Jasminum officinale
Common jasmine
○ ❖ SUMMER to AUTUMN

This is a pretty, summer-flowering climber, grown for its ferny foliage and highly fragrant, tubular flowers, which open into white stars. It looks lovely in a big ceramic container and can be trained over a trellis, obelisk or fence. Pinch out regularly to control the whippy growth. The flowers of 'Clotted Cream' (above) are an attractive creamy white.

Lonicera periclymenum
Honeysuckle
○ ◑ ❖ SPRING to AUTUMN

Honeysuckles are twining, woody climbers, with fragrant flowers carried in clusters from spring to autumn, depending on the type. Flower colour ranges from white through pale yellow to gold, pink and scarlet (above, 'Serotina'). The berries are attractive but poisonous. This species is ideal for a cottage-garden scheme and, being fragrant in the evening, perfectly complements roses (with their daytime scent).

Passiflora caerulea
Blue passion flower
○ ❄ ❖ SUMMER

This fast-growing plant climbs using twisting tendrils and often dies down for winter, re-emerging in spring. It flowers young, producing fat buds that open to show complex flowers, each up to 10cm (4in) across. Five white sepals and five white petals of equal length surround a circle of blue-purple filaments with a white band in the middle. Within this are five golden yellow anthers and three brown stigmas. The flowers are followed in hot summers by orange-yellow fruits. If you have room, grow it up a pergola.

Rhodochiton atrosanguineus
○ ❖ SUMMER to AUTUMN

Ideal for training up an obelisk in a large pot, the unusual flowers of this evergreen climber are truly eye-catching. They resemble delicate, deep-pink bells with elegant, narrow purple tubes hanging beneath them. The mid-green leaves are also attractively heart-shaped. In frost-prone areas, it is advisable to treat this plant as an annual.

Rosa Rose
○ ❖ SUMMER to AUTUMN

There are many climbing and rambling roses (including 'Albertine', above) that look wonderful growing up trellis against a warm wall, or up a pergola, an arch or an obelisk. They vary widely in flower shape, size and colour, fragrance, leaf colour and growth rate. Aim to match the rose to the situation – some of the rambling roses are very vigorous and will completely cover their supports. Roses like 'Little Rambler' are lovely if you are aiming for a cottage-garden effect, especially teamed with honeysuckle.

Thunbergia alata Black-eyed Susan
○ ✿ ❖SUMMER

This is an evergreen twining climber, although it is more often grown as an annual for a bright, colourful and exotic effect. The foliage is dense and mid-green and the flowers are orange-red, yellow or white with a chocolate-brown central eye. It thrives in a hot, sunny position, growing up a pergola or against a trellis, or it could trail from a hanging basket, but keep it well watered.

Tropaeolum speciosum
Flame creeper
○ ◑ pH ❖SUMMER

This exotic-looking form of nasturtium has deep-red flowers, produced from summer into autumn. Although it will tolerate full sun, when it's in a container it's easier to maintain in partial shade. This creeper likes moist, slightly acidic compost. It will trail up through a large conifer or, if you have a collection of acid-loving plants, a rhododendron.

Vitis coignetiae Crimson glory vine
○ ◑ ❖AUTUMN

The finest of all ornamental vines, the crimson glory vine is a vigorous climber with large, heart-shaped leaves that turn from mid-green to yellow, orange-red and then a striking crimson-purple colour in autumn. It looks superb scrambling over a yew or conifer hedge, bringing life to large expanses of green, or growing over a pergola. You'll need a hefty container to take the weight of this sizeable vine. The tiny, spherical, blue-black grapes, which are produced in autumn, are inedible.

Trachelospermum jasminoides
Star jasmine
○ ❖MID- to LATE SUMMER

The star jasmine is a twining climber with glossy, dark-green, oval leaves, turning bronze in winter. In summer, small clusters of highly fragrant white flowers open along the shoots and at the tips. Each has a cylindrical tube, flaring into twisted lobes. This plant thrives on a south-facing wall; put it near a window or door where you can fully appreciate the scent. It's a sun-lover that looks good in a ceramic pot for a Mediterranean effect.

Vitis Ornamental vine
○ ❖LATE SPRING to EARLY SUMMER

The ornamental vines are vigorous, woody climbers that support themselves with twining tendrils. They are ideal for covering a wall, fence or trellis. Several species are grown for their autumn colours of yellow, orange-red and eventually purple-crimson. Some produce small bunches of grapes in a hot, dry summer. Vines need large containers if they are to grow well and regular feeding if you want them to fruit. They are long-lived plants, so will need plenty of room for the roots, and their final container will need to be large and frost-proof.

Wisteria
○ ❖EARLY SUMMER

These hardy, deciduous climbers support themselves with twining stems. They have cascades of white, pink, purple or mauve, pea-like flowers. Their normal flowering season is late spring to midsummer, but small flushes may be produced until early autumn. They are ideal for covering walls, fences or trellis, or for training as standards. 'Amethyst Falls' (above), with fragrant flowers in early summer, is suitable for a container, but give it a large one – wisterias are greedy.

Clematis are great in containers. They're not difficult to grow but they do need a fair amount of TLC. Not all varieties are suited to growing in tubs, but those that are can bring a real touch of glamour to the container garden.

When you're choosing a pot for clematis, the main consideration is depth. Their roots grow down to escape the heat of the sun (which is why the plants you buy at the garden centre are usually in tall, narrow pots), so choose a container that gives the roots plenty of room. As a rule, the larger the pot, the happier the clematis. These plants are greedy so, in a relatively small pot, water and nutrient supplies will become depleted very quickly and, before you know it, you'll be thinking you spend more time feeding and watering the thing than you do enjoying it.

Clematis are very versatile in that they're happy to grow sideways, along low walls or over tree stumps, as well as up walls, fences and into trees. If you use an obelisk or small trellis for support, they can be kept fairly compact; if you provide wires along walls, you can encourage them to branch out and really do themselves proud. Decide how you want them to fit into your scheme, then give them what they need to repay your efforts.

① 'Jackmanii Superba' produces large, deep-purple blooms from midsummer to early autumn.
② 'Etoile Rose' has small, nodding, bell-shaped, deep-pink flowers from early or midsummer to autumn.
③ 'Purpurea Plena Elegans' has double, dusky red-purple flowers from midsummer to early autumn.
④ 'Elizabeth', one of the montana group, produces pale-pink, scented flowers in late spring.
⑤ 'Bill MacKenzie' has small, bell-shaped yellow flowers from midsummer to late autumn.

Don't forget

Most clematis are happiest when their heads are warm and their feet are cool – flowers in sunlight, roots in shade. Site the tub in a good, light position and add a layer of pebbles or similar topping (*see* page 30) over the compost to protect the delicate roots from sun as well as frost. One trick is to place the pot inside another, larger pot, filling the space between the two with pebbles or other insulation material. Then cover the lot with your chosen topping. Do not allow clematis to become waterlogged.

Perennials

Perennials are plants that live from one year to the next, but most are herbaceous, dying down in winter. With a few exceptions, such as hellebores, those that don't die back and overwinter below ground tend to be those with woody stems. So, if you want your container garden to look good in winter, include different types from the wide selection on offer.

Anemone × hybrida
Japanese anemone
○ ◑ ❖ MIDSUMMER to AUTUMN

Japanese anemone cultivars (above, 'Honorine Jobert') provide a fine display of colour from mid- or late summer to the first frosts. They produce tall, branching stems of saucer-shaped flowers in white and shades of pink, with a central tuft of yellow stamens. Divide and repot every two or three years.

Aeonium 'Zwartkop'
◑ ▦ ❖ SPRING

This unusual succulent has upright stems, each bearing a rosette of almost black leaves. It needs dappled shade or the leaves will scorch, and well-drained compost, preferring to almost dry out between waterings. It has yellow flowers in spring. This plant is ideal for a black garden or monochrome display.

Ajuga reptans
Bugle
◑ ● ❖ SUMMER

Ajugas are invaluable for providing a low, spreading mat of evergreen foliage, with the bonus of flowers in spring. 'Black Scallop' (above) has luscious, dark-purple leaves – a striking foil for other plants – and spires of mauve-blue flowers. 'Burgundy Glow' has grey-green leaves marked pink and cream, and blue flowers. Ajugas are happy in shade and like a bit of moisture, so don't let the container dry out.

Anthriscus sylvestris 'Ravenswing'
Black Queen Anne's lace
○ ◑ ❖ SPRING to SUMMER

Black Queen Anne's lace is a clump-forming, short-lived perennial with masses of lacy, dark purple-brown leaves and clouds of tiny, pinkish-white flowers in late spring and early summer. Plant it in a pot on its own where it can grow to full size and show itself to best effect. Like many other dark-leaved plants, the colour of the foliage is considerably better in partial shade than in full sun. It sets plenty of seed for future sowings, but be selective and keep only the darkest seedlings.

Agave americana
○ ▦ ❖ SUMMER

This succulent makes a spectacular specimen plant for a hot area. It has long, fleshy, grey-green leaves with toothed edges and spiny tips. Clusters of funnel-shaped, greenish-yellow flowers appear on smooth stems from the centre of the rosette. Each rosette flowers once, then dies off, leaving new offsets to replace it. This is an architectural perennial that needs room to grow.

Alternanthera dentata 'Purple Knight'
◑ ▦ ❖ SUMMER

A relatively new introduction and a dramatic addition to the list of almost-black plants, this is a perennial foliage plant with an upright habit and spreading stems. It can be used to underplant a mixed container or on its own for a striking effect in partial shade.

Briza media Quaking grass
○ ❖ SUMMER

The quaking grass is ideal for containers and forms a perennial clump of blue-green leaves. From late spring until midsummer, it produces upright stems bearing heart-shaped spikelets. These are green, tinted purple as they open, becoming straw-coloured with age, and are shaped like a rattlesnake's tail. Their great attraction is the way they dance and rattle together in the breeze, adding sound to your collection of grasses. Dry them and use in indoor arrangements.

Carex 'Amazon Mist' Sedge
○ ❖ SUMMER

Sedge is a clump-forming perennial grass that is ideal for use in a container, particularly growing on its own as a specimen, where you can appreciate it from all sides. 'Amazon Mist' (above) has lush, silver-green foliage with a lax habit and twisting tips. It adds an ethereal, misty appearance and an interesting texture to a mixed display, especially if positioned at the front where it will help hide other pots.

Cosmos atrosanguineus
Chocolate plant
○ ✿ ❖ SUMMER to AUTUMN

This plant earns its name from the chocolate scent of its velvety, saucer-shaped, deep-red flowers. It is likely to be killed off by frost without protection, so in frost-prone areas lift the tuber and store it almost dry in a frost-free place until spring. Regular dead-heading helps to ensure flowers until autumn. Put chocolate plants close to seating areas, so you can enjoy their scent on warm, still days.

Brunnera macrophylla 'Jack Frost'
◐ ❖ SPRING to SUMMER

This brunnera is an invaluable plant for a shady spot, with large, heart-shaped, hairy leaves that are shunned by slugs and snails and stay looking good throughout summer. Dainty, blue forget-me-not flowers (sometimes white) open very early in spring, before the leaves emerge. Some cultivars have plain green leaves, others are spotted or edged with creamy white, but the most desirable is 'Jack Frost' (above), with the surface of the leaves being almost completely covered in silver.

Cordyline australis
New Zealand cabbage palm
○ ◐ ❄ ❖ SUMMER

Cordylines are evergreen, spiky-leaved perennials with arching, lance-shaped leaves. They look very striking in a pot, and will eventually grow to resemble a woody-stemmed, palm-like tree; the leaves grow to about 60cm (24in) long. The flowers, which are produced on mature plants in long clusters, are sweetly fragrant and cup-shaped, followed in hot summers by round white berries. Several cultivars are available with colourful foliage, so choose one to complement your colour scheme.

Dianthus Pink
○ ❖ SUMMER

Pinks are attractive, evergreen, sun-loving plants that prefer alkaline conditions and grow to form cushion-like mounds of silver-grey foliage. The flowers are delicately sweet- or clove-scented and brightly coloured in white and shades of pink to dark red. They may be single, semi-double or double and are wonderful as cut flowers. Dead-head to prevent seed formation and encourage repeat flowering. Sizes vary from tiny alpine forms to taller varieties like 'Mrs Sinkins' and 'Doris', which have long been cottage-garden favourites.

Dicentra spectabilis
Bleeding heart
◑ ● ❖SPRING

This clump-forming perennial has tall, arching stems and pale-green leaves. In spring, it produces delicate, hanging, heart-shaped flowers with rose-pink outer petals and white inner ones. There is also a white-flowered form, 'Alba'. The ferny foliage is pretty once the flowers have finished, and this is a good plant for a partially shaded area. It is deep-rooted and, ideally, needs a container to itself.

Eryngium alpinum Sea holly
○ ❖SUMMER

The sea holly is a rosette-forming perennial that can tolerate a sunny, dry position and coastal winds as long as it doesn't become waterlogged. It has spiny basal leaves of mid-green, steely-blue flowering shoots and thistle-like flowers. It's a good plant for an exposed site such as a sunny balcony.

Gaura lindheimeri
○ ◑ ❖LATE SPRING to AUTUMN

Sometimes treated as an annual, this gaura produces tall, upright stems of short-lived white flowers with four petals and long stamens. They are pink in bud, open white in the morning, fade to pink and die off by the evening, to be replaced the next morning. It is a graceful addition to a collection of container plants, as the flowers dance in the breeze. Placed among lower-growing plants, the flowers will rise above the foliage and add a misty height to the display.

Eragrostis elliottii 'Wind Dancer'
Love grass
○ ❖SUMMER

This hardy perennial grass has sea-green foliage that falls and curls over the edge of the container, so it can be planted in the middle of other plants (like bedding) for a misty effect. The colder the climate in which it's grown, the more upright the foliage will be. The white flowers begin to appear in summer, but carry on blooming throughout autumn. It is a rather unruly plant, but very effective in an informal planting.

Festuca glauca Blue fescue
○ ❖SUMMER

This is a thick, tufty, evergreen perennial grass of a glorious blue-grey. The leaves are straight, upright and slender, making it a good plant to use to complement silver heathers (Calluna), or to set in a silver or black container on its own to make a focal point. The flowers are produced in summer and are blue-green, flushed violet.

Helleborus × hybridus
Hellebore, Lenten rose
◑ ◑ ● ❖WINTER to SPRING

Most hellebores are fully hardy and provide a wonderful display of foliage and flowers throughout late winter and early spring. Lenten roses, or hybrid hellebores (H. × hybridus) have flowers in a wide range of rich colours from white, shades of cream, yellow, green, pink, reddish and purple through to almost black, with prominent yellow stamens. These are good plants for a partially shaded area and add interest during winter.

Heuchera
◯ ◑ ❖SUMMER

These clump-forming, semi-evergreen perennials (evergreen in milder climates) are grown as much for their foliage as their flowers. As they grow, they form a mound of attractive, wide, heart-shaped leaves of green, bronze, caramel, pinkish or purple, prized by flower arrangers. The flowers are tiny, in loose clusters on tall, upright stems and are attractive to bees. New varieties are being added every year, so you should find a colour to suit almost any scheme. Some darker heucheras bleach slightly in full sun.

Hosta Plantain lily
◑ ● ❖SUMMER

Hostas are long-lived perennials that form a mass of long, rounded or heart-shaped leaves in a range of sizes and colours from dark green to golden or blue-grey, often with markings of white, cream or yellow. Tall, upright stems carry trumpet-shaped, pendulous flowers in white or mauve, sometimes with a delicate fragrance. Golden-leaved forms (above, 'Gold Standard') need some sun to maintain their colour but on the whole hostas are better shaded from midday sun.

Juncus effusus f. spiralis
Corkscrew rush
◑ pH↓ ❖SUMMER

The corkscrew rush, an unusually shaped, grass-like plant, forms a dense clump of stems that twist and spiral into a mass of coils. It prefers to remain damp at all times, so it's easier to maintain in a shady position, where it can be used as a focal point in a raised pot. It likes acid compost. In up to 8cm (3in) of water it can be used as a pond plant, or as a bog plant in very damp compost.

Juncus inflexus
◯ ◑ pH↓ ❖SUMMER

This is similar in growing preferences to *J. effusus* f. *spiralis* and can be grown along with it in a shady spot. 'Afro' has spiralling, matt-blue stems and 'Blue Arrow' has stiffly upright, blue foliage that looks good combined with other acid-loving plants, such as heathers. Like *J. effusus* (top) it can also be used as a pond plant in up to 8cm (3in) of water, or a bog plant in very damp compost.

Liriope muscari
◑ ● pH↓ ❖AUTUMN

This unusual, grass-like tuberous perennial (actually a member of the lily family) forms a dense clump of dark-green leaves that look architectural in their own right, but it comes into its own in autumn when the dense spikes of bright violet flowers appear above the leaves. These look almost artificial, they are so intense. Liriopes combine well with pieris, rhododendrons and heathers, adding colour in late summer and autumn. Use ericaceous compost and position the container in shade.

Luzula nivea Snowy woodrush
◯ ❖SUMMER

The snowy woodrush is a loosely tufted, evergreen perennial with deep-green leaves. It is grown primarily for its attractive flowers, which are a shiny pure white and produced in tight clusters from early to midsummer. They can be dried for use in indoor arrangements. This plant makes an attractive addition to a collection of grasses or can be added to a mixed display for texture.

Lychnis × haageana
○ ◐ ❖ SUMMER

Although this plant is normally treated as an annual, it's actually perennial and should live through all but the coldest winters. It usually has green foliage, but the new Lumina Bronze Leaf series contains a stunning dark-leaved form (above), with bronze foliage and large dark-red flowers. The bronze form combines well with the 'Mocca' begonias to bring a rich splash of colour to a collection of dark-leaved plants.

Melica transsilvanica 'Red Spire'
○ pH↓ ❖ SUMMER

A deciduous perennial grass, this plant forms a tufted clump of mid-green leaves and flowers in its first year. It is grown primarily for its spectacular flowers, which are reddish brown and borne in long, satiny spires in early summer. This is a tall plant that likes a hot spot in full sun, and a container with good drainage and acid compost.

Ophiopogon planiscapus 'Nigrescens'
○ ◐ pH↓ ❖ SUMMER

Dramatic and striking, this can be grown in a pot on its own, or combined with other plants. It is a rhizomatous perennial with grass-like leaves that grows slowly to form a dense clump, but the unusual feature is the almost black foliage. Short stems of bell-shaped, purplish-white flowers are produced on this member of the lily family, followed by blackish fruits. It prefers slightly acid compost.

Phormium tenax
New Zealand flax
○ ◐ ❖ SUMMER

This striking, clump-forming perennial has long, rigid, blade-like leaves in various colours. 'Veitchianum' has broad, creamy-white striped foliage; 'Chocolate Dream' is a deep chocolate-bronze; 'All Black' and 'Deep Purple' have lovely dark leaves. It is a large, architectural plant and really needs to be seen in isolation rather than as part of a display, so you can appreciate the foliage from all sides. It produces a tall flower spike of red flowers in summer but is mainly grown for its leaves.

Phyllostachys nigra Black bamboo
○ ◐ ● ❖ YEAR-ROUND

The black bamboo is a stunning specimen plant that will slowly grow to form a dramatic clump in a large container. It has slender, arching stems that age from mid-green to glossy black in their second or third year. The leaves are also dark green, on stems that branch as they age, so it is also useful as a summer windbreak, although cold winds can damage the foliage. Make sure you use a loam-based compost, such as John Innes No. 3, because bamboos are generally hungry plants. Feed and water regularly, and divide the plant when it outgrows its container.

Pulsatilla vulgaris Pasque flower
○ ❖ SPRING

This is a very pretty, clump-forming, alpine-like perennial for a small container, with finely divided, ferny leaves. In spring, it has bell-shaped flowers covered in silky hairs, in dark purple, violet, red or white, according to the variety. It likes very good drainage (so add grit to the compost) and dislikes root disturbance, so plant it young and leave it alone until repotting is absolutely necessary.

Saxifraga Saxifrage
○ ◑ ❖ SPRING

A large, diverse group of plants, there are many attractive, low-growing species for containers. The alpine types are ideal for well-drained troughs and individual pots. Some form rosettes, others are mossy-looking or have an unusual white encrustation of lime on the leaves. They produce a mass of cup-shaped pink, yellow or white flowers in spring and early summer, but cannot tolerate wet, so keep them well drained by adding extra grit to the compost.

Sempervivum Houseleek
○ ❖ SUMMER

This is a group of mat-forming, succulent perennials that thrive in full sun and poor, well-drained soil, so they are ideal for a sun-baked patio, balcony or steps. Some have a cobweb-like covering of fine white hairs or attractive, reddish leaf coloration. As the plant matures, a rosette will produce a flower spike of star-shaped white, yellow, pink or red flowers, but then it dies off, to be replaced by new, smaller rosettes around the edge.

Stipa tenuissima
○ ❖ SUMMER

This perennial grass forms a dense clump of upright, bright-green foliage that will fountain up from the top of a narrow container. In summer, it produces feathery, greenish-white flowers that age to buff. They are so fine, they look like a cloud and willl move gracefully in the slightest breeze. This is a wonderful plant for texture in a mixed display.

Sedum spectabile Ice plant
○ ❖ LATE SUMMER to AUTUMN

There are many forms of hardy Sedum, ranging from small alpines to this larger deciduous, clump-forming perennial. It has rounded, succulent-looking leaves on upright stems that bear huge, flattened flowerheads from late summer into autumn. These may be white (as in 'Iceberg', above) or pale pink through to dark red, depending on the variety. Both butterflies and bees love them, so it is a useful plant if you want to attract wildlife to the garden.

Stipa gigantea Golden oat
○ ❖ SUMMER

One of the tallest grasses when it flowers, this densely tufted evergreen (or semi-evergreen) perennial really needs a container to itself. In summer, it produces bristled, silvery purplish-green spikelets that resemble oats and wave in the slightest breeze. They turn a glorious gold as they ripen and can be dried for use in the house.

Veronica spicata
○ ◑ ❖ SUMMER

Erect stems bear distinctive flower spikes in shades of blue, violet, pink or white (above, 'Snow White'). The foliage is normally mid-green, but also occasionally gold or silver-grey. This mat-forming, low-growing plant is particularly good for containers, surrounding a taller central occupant.

Bulbs

Think bulbs and you almost immediately think of spring flowers. It's true that there are more bulbs for spring than there are for any other season, but bulbs (including corms, tubers and rhizomes) comprise a large group of plants, and the summer-flowering ones (such as lilies and agapanthus) are often more dramatic.

Agapanthus campanulatus
African lily
○ ❀ ❖ SUMMER to AUTUMN

This deciduous, clump-forming perennial has arching leaves and globe-shaped clusters of blue or white flowers carried on tall stems. The individual bell- or trumpet-shaped flowers are held aloft or droop down. The variegated form is not frost hardy.

Allium cristophii Star of Persia
○ ❖ EARLY SUMMER to AUTUMN

This bulbous perennial is a member of the onion family. It has grey-green leaves and the pinkish-purple, metallic-looking flowers are produced in a huge, globe-shaped head. The heads dry well and look good in vases.

Anemone blanda
○ ◑ ❖ LATE WINTER to EARLY SPRING

This is a clump-forming, tuberous perennial with a creeping habit. It produces deeply lobed, dark-green leaves just above the compost on thin, wiry, dark- or bluish-green stems. The single flowers are available in white, pink and deep blue. These little plants are ideal as early season interest in a pot or at the base of a tree or shrub.

Colchicum Autumn crocus
○ ❖ AUTUMN

These crocus-like, cormous perennials produce showy, goblet-shaped, pink, violet or white flowers (as in *C. speciosum* 'Album', above) in autumn. They flower without foliage – the strap-like leaves do not appear until the following spring. Repot every four to five years in summer.

Crocus
○ ◑ ❖ EARLY to MID-SPRING or AUTUMN

These familiar small perennials grow from individual corms, producing long, slender leaves, often with a white-striped upper surface. The flowers are goblet-shaped, four or more per corm, in shades of white, yellow, orange, blue or purple (above, *C. tommasinianus* 'Whitewell Purple'), plain or striped. Grow them on their own in a pot, or use them in a mixed bulb planting or with a tree or shrub to extend the season of interest.

Cyclamen Sow bread
◑ ❖ AUTUMN to SPRING

By using both *C. hederifolium* (autumn) and *C. coum* (winter) you can have cyclamen in flower through most of the winter. Both are tuberous perennials that produce rounded leaves and nodding (sometimes fragrant) flowers with reflexed petals in white and shades of pink and red. Cyclamen can be underplanted with another plant, preferably in a large pot that will not be disturbed too often. Plant with the upper third of the bulb visible above the surface.

Eranthis hyemalis Winter aconite
○ ◐ ❖WINTER

The winter aconite provides a welcome splash of colour in winter with its bright-yellow, buttercup-like flowers set amid mid-green foliage. It is a clump-forming, tuberous perennial that prefers neutral to alkaline conditions and will eventually spread to fill its container. Winter aconites can be added to containers of trees or shrubs as long as these are not acid-lovers.

Fritillaria Fritillary
○ ❖MID- to LATE SPRING

A varied group of pretty, bulbous perennials with bell-shaped, often highly patterned flowers, ranging from very small species such as *F. michailovskyi*, at 10cm (4in) high, through to the imposing *F. imperialis* (crown imperial), which can reach 1.5m (5ft) high. Perhaps the most striking is *F. meleagris* (the snake's head fritillary, above), with its nodding, chequered mauve and white flowers. Fritillaries are intolerant of excess moisture, so add grit to the compost and protect pots from severe frost.

Galanthus nivalis
Common snowdrop
◐ ❖LATE WINTER to SPRING

The snowdrop is a hardy, clump-forming, low-growing, bulbous perennial that produces flat, strap-shaped leaves and drooping white flowers, often marked with green on the inner tepals. It is ideal for planting under an established tree or shrub in a container, as it dies down and becomes dormant during summer and autumn, so will not compete for water. A pot full of snowdrops looks lovely on an outdoor table, or in a traditional cottage-garden display.

Hedychium gardnerianum
Kahili ginger
◐ ▨ ❖SUMMER

This ginger lily provides an unusual focal point with its large, lush foliage and tall spikes of exotic-looking flowers. It prefers to grow among other plants that give it a little shade and shelter from cold winds. The individual flowers are tubular, fragrant and white, yellow or reddish orange. Its exotic appearance goes well in a tropical display with a plant like *Canna*.

Hyacinthus orientalis Hyacinth
○ ◐ ❖SPRING

Cultivars of this hyacinth are grown for their brightly coloured, highly scented, waxy flowers. They are bell-shaped, single or double, and come in shades of white (as in 'Carnegie', above), yellow, pink, orange, red and blue, in clusters of up to 40 on a single broad, upright stem amid bright green, strap-like leaves. Keep a pot near a door or window that you open regularly so that you can appreciate the heavy scent from indoors.

Iris
○ ◐ ❖LATE WINTER to MIDSUMMER

Bulbous irises have deciduous, lance-shaped leaves and beardless flowers, and are dormant in summer. There are three groups: Reticulata, with blue, white or red-purple flowers; Juno, with colourful 'fall' petals and small 'standard' petals; and Xiphium (including Dutch, English and Spanish irises), with blue, lavender, yellow or white flowers. Smaller varieties are ideal in an alpine collection for interest early in the season. Reticulata irises (above, 'Harmony') produce square-shaped leaves and flowers in late winter to early spring.

Lilium Lily
○ ◐ ❀ (some species) ❖ SUMMER to AUTUMN

There are about 100 different kinds of lily, varying in height and flower size, shape and colour (and hardiness). The bulb is made up of fleshy white or yellow scales. The flowers are trumpet-shaped and very fragrant, with six petals that curl into an open star shape, ranging from 2.5cm (1in) to 25cm (10in) across, depending on variety. Lilies (above, 'Peace') are tall, but take up little room at the base, so you can stand them among other plants to add height to a display.

Narcissus Daffodil
○ ◐ ❖ SPRING

This is a big group of spring-flowering bulbs that range from dwarf types (above, 'Tête à Tête') to tall varieties. The flowers have an inner trumpet and an outer row of petals. Shades include yellow, white, orange, cream and pink; they are solitary or grow in clusters, have single or double petals and have trumpets that vary in shape and length. Choose different varieties with a succession of flowering times, and you can have daffodils in flower for three to four months.

Nerine bowdenii
○ ❖ AUTUMN

This is a bulbous perennial for a hot spot at the base of a sunny wall. It likes good drainage and flowers best if the pot is very full. It produces broad, strap-like leaves and flower spikes of funnel-shaped, pink flowers with a slight fragrance. There is also a white form. This is a spectacular plant for colour in late summer and early autumn and, as the leaves are not particularly showy, it is ideal for growing through low-growing plants to add height and interest.

Scilla siberica Siberian squill
○ ◐ ❖ SPRING

The Siberian squill is a small, dainty bulb grown for its nodding, bright-blue flowers, carried in clusters of four to five on dark-green stems. The flower buds emerge at the same time as the long, slender leaves in early spring, and flowering normally continues for several weeks, but is better when the bulbs are not disturbed. This pretty little plant is ideal for an alpine collection or table-top display, where you can see the flowers; it blends well in a cottage garden.

Tulipa Tulip
○ ❖ SPRING

Tulip flowers may be single, double, goblet- or star-shaped, fringed, or long and slender. Shades include white, yellow, pink, red (above, 'Red Georgette'), orange, and purple to almost black. Bulbs can be left in the container year-round or lifted and stored in a cool place, but for best results it is often better to plant new bulbs each year. They prefer shelter from strong winds. Tulips flower from early to late spring, depending on the variety, and vary in height from 25cm (10in), such as T. kaufmanniana, to around 60cm (24in), like T. 'Apeldoorn'. If you combine several forms, you could have a succession of flowers. The smaller, spreading varieties need room to expand sideways. Grow each type in its own pot so that it can be brought into a display as it comes into bud and removed when the flowers fade.

Don't forget

A container full of bulbs is always a cheery sight in itself, but remember that bulbs are also very useful for underplanting pot-grown deciduous trees or shrubs – some carefully chosen bulbs will provide colour and interest in a season when the main specimen plant is taking a break.

Annuals and tender perennials

Annuals are ideally suited to containers because there's no need to worry about repotting them, and many can be sown directly into the pot in which they will flower – saving valuable growing space. In cool climates, some perennials, such as pelargoniums, are classed as annuals because they won't last the winter outdoors, but keep them somewhere warm and they will last from year to year.

Argyranthemum
○ ❀ ❖SUMMER to AUTUMN

These evergreen sub-shrubs, usually treated as annuals, have ferny foliage (which varies from mid- to blue-green) and pretty, daisy-like flowers in white, yellow (as in 'Jamaica Primrose', above) or pink. In spring, pinch out growing tips to encourage bushiness, and dead-head regularly to maintain flowering. Useful on a hot patio, they are low maintenance and tolerate exposure to salty winds.

Begonia semperflorens
◑ ❀ ❖SUMMER to AUTUMN

This compact, versatile, profusely flowering begonia has glossy, fleshy foliage that is mid-green to dark bronze; flowers are usually single, in white or shades of red and pink. It is one of the few bedding plants to prefer a little shade (direct sunlight can cause scorching). It is also low maintenance.

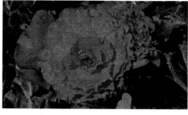

Begonia × *tuberhybrida* Mocca series
◑ ❀ ❖SUMMER

This unusually dark-leaved group of tuberous begonias will tolerate all but midday sun. The dark chocolate-bronze foliage will complement any collection of dark-leaved plants, and the flowers are rich, dark red, orange, pink or yellow. The pure white-flowered form would fit well into a monochrome display.

Bellis perennis Daisy
○ ◑ ❖SPRING to SUMMER

The bedding daisy is a hardy, rosette-forming perennial that will grow in most situations. It has bright-green leaves and long-stalked flowers, borne singly throughout spring and summer. The flowers may be single or double, in white and shades of red, rose and pink with yellow centres. This reliable little plant is one of the best for colour in almost any season, as it will often go through winter.

Brugmansia Angel's trumpet
○ ❀ ❖SUMMER to AUTUMN

These are exotic-looking, large specimen plants for a warm, sheltered terrace in summer. They are grown for their big, showy, trumpet-shaped flowers, which range in colour from white to yellow, orange (as in *B. sanguinea*, above), or pink. Water generously when in full growth and use free-draining compost. Many are heavily scented so put them in a large pot near a seating area. Over-winter them indoors by a sunny window.

Canna Indian shot
○ ❀ ❖SUMMER to AUTUMN

These highly striking, rhizomatous herbaceous perennials are usually grown as summer bedding in a hot spot for an exotic effect, as they seldom survive a winter outdoors. The leaves are large and blade-shaped, varying from green to dark bronze, often with marked veins. The flowers are tubular, flaring out as three wide petals, in vibrant reds, yellows and oranges (as in 'Wyoming', above), with long stamens. They combine well with ginger lilies. Take care to buy virus-free stock since many are badly infected.

Capsicum annuum 'Black Pearl'
○ ◐ ❋ ❖SUMMER

This is a stunning, black-leaved form of ornamental pepper for your collection of black-leaved plants. It forms a bushy, upright, multi-branched plant with foliage that is green at first, but matures to glossy black. It produces small, shiny black fruits that finally mature to deep red. Peppers prefer high humidity, so plant them in a wide container with other plants around the base.

Ensete ventricosum
Ornamental banana
○ ◐ ❋ ❖SUMMER

This ornamental banana plant has long, blade-shaped leaves with a broad red midrib. In a warm summer, cup-shaped white flowers surrounded by red bracts may be followed by banana-like fruit (although these are usually too dry to eat). It makes a superb specimen plant or gives a wonderful sub-tropical effect to a mixed planting.

Helianthus annuus Sunflower
○ ❋ ❖SUMMER

The annual sunflower comes in all sizes and shades of yellow (as in 'Valentine', above), bronze and brownish red. The shorter, multi-stemmed varieties are the most suitable for containers, and some excellent ones can be raised from seed. They have coarse, heart-shaped leaves, hairy stems and flowers with outer ray florets (usually yellow) and inner disc florets (yellow, brown or purple).

Dahlia
○ ❋ ❖SUMMER to AUTUMN

Bedding varieties of dahlia are smaller than the types grown for show or cutting, and form compact plants with green or bronze foliage and flowers of white, yellow, orange, red or bronze. They are resilient plants for your display and will flower from midsummer until the first frosts if you dead-head regularly. The dry tubers are often sold in mixed packs, making colour choice difficult, so it may be best to buy the plants in flower to make sure you get the right ones.

Gazania
○ ❋ ❖SUMMER

Gazanias are sun-lovers that make a fantastic splash of colour. They tolerate coastal conditions, full sun and being slightly dry, so are relatively easy. The leaf shape varies between forms, but they are usually covered with soft, silver-grey hairs, giving them a silvery appearance. The flowers, which close in dull weather, are large and daisy-like in yellow, orange or red and sometimes zoned in a contrasting colour (as above, 'Blackberry Ripple'). Pots by a sunny front door make a welcoming sight.

Heliotropium arborescens
Cherry pie, Heliotrope
○ ❋ ❖SUMMER

This is a bushy, short-lived shrub (above, 'Chatsworth'), usually treated as an annual, and known as cherry pie because of the sweet, fruity fragrance of its striking, purplish-blue flowers, which are attractive to butterflies. The rough, deeply veined leaves are often tinted purple. It is an ideal plant for containers and works very well with white flowers, such as pelargoniums, for a cool but striking effect.

Impatiens walleriana Busy lizzie
◐ ❀ ❖SUMMER to AUTUMN

Reliable and tolerant, this busy lizzie will flower throughout the summer, especially in a sheltered, partially shady spot. It flowers from a young age, producing clusters of spurred blooms on succulent-looking stems amid lush foliage. There are many types and colour mixtures to choose from, including white, pinks, reds, oranges and purples. It is unlikely to need dead-heading, as it seldom sets seed. A good front-of-display plant and also ideal around the base of a tree or shrub.

Lathyrus odoratus Sweet pea
○ ❖SUMMER

The sweet pea is a cottage-garden favourite and several dwarf forms have been bred that are ideal for growing in containers. They are low-growing and will trail if not given support, with flowers in shades of white, pink, red and blue, borne in clusters and heavily scented (especially in the evening). Picking regularly or removing dead flowers before they can set seed ensures a succession of flowers. New forms include seed-raised *L. belinensis*, with two-tone, orange-yellow flowers.

Lobelia erinus
○ ◐ ❀ ❖SUMMER to AUTUMN

This popular bushy or trailing plant is used in bedding schemes and baskets everywhere, because it is a good, reliable filler with masses of flowers, provided you keep it well fed and watered. The flowers may be purple, blue, carmine, pink or white and the leaves green or bronze. Trailing forms are attractive spilling over the edge of a hanging basket or window box, especially in a sheltered spot, as they can scorch in cold winds.

Iresine herbstii 'Purple Lady'
○ ◐ ❀ ❖SUMMER

There are several bright-pink forms of *Iresine*, grown for their stem and leaf colour rather than their insignificant flowers. This is the darkest form yet and, especially when it is grown in some shade, the whole plant is a rich deep purple. It is ideal for a mixed container, as it is low-growing and will spread, cascading down the sides as the stems get longer and heavier. It is dark enough to use in a black-leaved garden as long as there is some shade.

Leucanthemum × superbum
○ ◐ ❀ ❖SUMMER to AUTUMN

This pretty daisy is sold as both an annual and a perennial because it will live through the winter as long as you keep the crown away from excess moisture. Throughout summer, it produces flowers on tall stems that are good for cutting. The flowers may be single or double, and have golden or pale-yellow centres. This is a good plant for adding interest to the centre of a mixed display as the flowers rise up above the foliage.

Nicotiana × sanderae
Tobacco plant
○ ◐ ❀ ❖SUMMER

An ornamental relative of the tobacco plant, this is a multi-branched annual with a low rosette of leaves and a tall flowering stem. It can reach 1m (40in) tall and has densely packed clusters of sweet-smelling white (as in 'Albus', above), pink, red or purple flowers in summer, which tend to open during the evening and close in very bright sunlight. Position this plant where you sit in the evenings to make the most of the scent.

Pelargonium
○ ◑ ✿ ❖ SUMMER to AUTUMN

Commonly (but incorrectly) known as geraniums, these bushy plants have bright, attractive flowers and/or scented foliage. Flower colours include red, salmon, pink, violet and white. Regal pelargoniums (such as 'Aztec') are bushy, evergreen perennials with whiskery leaves. The flowers are large, in one colour or combined shades of white, pink, salmon, orange, red or purple. They are usually single, and the upper petals are often blotched with a darker colour. Scented-leaf pelargoniums (such as 'Graveolens', above) tend to have small flowers, with finely cut, toothed or lobed foliage. The range of leaf scents includes lemon, peppermint, orange, lime and balm. Zonal pelargoniums (such as 'Frank Headley', top) have big, rounded leaves, sometimes variegated or marked with a darker, horseshoe shape. The flowers may be single, semi-double or double, in white and shades of orange, pink, red or purple. The zonals demand full sun if they are not to become leggy. The scented-leaf and regal types are happy in dappled light.

Pennisetum glaucum
○ ◑ ❄ ❖ SUMMER

Two forms of this millet are ideal for using in a dark-leaved display: 'Purple Majesty' and the slightly shorter 'Purple Baron'. Both have rich, dark purple-bronze foliage that is a better colour if the plant is in full sun (in shade, it turns a little more green). Use them as a centrepiece in a mixed container, as a screen or as specimen plants grown singly in large containers. Both are half-hardy perennials, so may be better grown as annuals each year.

Petunia
○ ◑ ✿ ❖ SUMMER to AUTUMN

Petunias are colourful plants with wide, single or double, trumpet-shaped flowers throughout summer and mid-green leaves. They may be bushy or trailing in habit. Flower colours include white, cream, yellow, pink, red, mauve, blue, purple and a range of striped forms. Newer introductions are self-cleaning, which means you no longer have to remove the dead flowers. The Surfinia series and Wave series of bedding petunias flower profusely throughout the season.

Primula
○ ◑ ✿ ❖ AUTUMN/WINTER/SPRING

This is a large group of plants, including primrose and polyanthus. All are tough and reliable, with wide-flaring, funnel-shaped flowers and a basal rosette of rough leaves. There are bedding varieties that flower from autumn throughout winter if it's mild. Primulas are reliable for colour – white, yellow, pink, purple and red (above, Cowichan Garnet Group) – but you need to keep the slugs off. Many are fragrant. They also suit hanging baskets, window boxes and troughs.

Salvia farinacea 'Victoria'
Mealy sage
○ ◑ ✿ ❖ SUMMER to AUTUMN

This is a popular salvia, ideal for a pot or container, being compact but bushy in habit. It is perennial but is normally grown as an annual. It has attractive, pointed, grey-green leaves and erect, slim flower spikes that open to a deep indigo blue.

Solenostemon scutellarioides
Coleus
○ ◐ ❄ ❖SUMMER

Coleus was once the staple of the summer container, but fell from favour. Who knows why, when it offers such a huge range of foliage colours? One new form is 'Chocolate Mint', with large leaves of a rich chocolate brown edged with mint green, making it ideal for the dark-leaved collection. Another is the Kong series of four forms with some of the largest leaves available for bedding. Overwinter coleus indoors or treat it as an annual.

Tagetes Marigold
○ ❖SUMMER to AUTUMN

Marigolds are grown for their glorious, hot flower colours of yellow, gold, orange and mahogany-red. Single and double varieties are available, the singles being daisy-like, sometimes with a darker eye or coloured splash on the petals.
T. erecta (African marigold, above) is tall, with big, rounded flowers in yellow and orange, ideal for the centre of a display.
T. patula (French marigold) is shorter and bushier, and better suited to the front of a display. Dead-head regularly.

Tropaeolum majus Nasturtium
○ ◐ ❖SUMMER to AUTUMN

Fast-growing with a climbing or trailing habit, nasturtiums are deservedly popular for their brightly coloured flowers. Ideal for training up a support, such as an obelisk, or for trailing over a tall container, the vibrant yellow, orange to deep-red trumpet-shaped blooms stand out beautifully against rounded leaves that can be pale to mid-green, purple-green or marbled. Give them a free-draining compost and keep moist when in flower. The roots prefer shade.

Verbena × hybrida
○ ❖SUMMER to AUTUMN

This plant may be bushy or trailing and is ideal for containers of all kinds. Clusters of small, fragrant flowers are produced from summer until the first frosts in white, pinks, reds, blues, lilacs and purples. Dead-head regularly for continued flowering. White verbenas have a cooling effect and are useful for blurring the edges of the display (as well as hiding the container), especially when trailing from a trough or window box.

Viola Pansy, viola
○ ◐ ❖YEAR-ROUND

This group includes large-flowered pansies and small-flowered violas, both of which have become the staple of the container all year round. New varieties are completely hardy and continue to flower in all but the very coldest weather, especially if they have some shelter. In fact, they are more likely to take a rest in the heat of summer. The colour range includes lemon, gold, yellow, red, white, blue and deep violet, sometimes with darker markings.

Zinnia
○ ❖SUMMER

Pretty, bushy plants with branched stems and mid-green, lance-shaped leaves, they bear colourful, single or semi-double flowers in white, yellow, pink, red, bright orange, magenta, purple and a spectacular lime green. There are also bicolours in shades of purple, red, brown, orange and yellow. The taller zinnias are excellent for cutting.

Fruit and vegetables

It's getting easier and easier to grow fruit and veg in containers, but choose the small, quick-maturing varieties recommended for pots. The number of these varieties is increasing, and much of this 'mini-veg' can be ready to eat in 6 to 12 weeks. Yields may not be huge, but the things you grow will taste so much better than shop-bought produce because they're so fresh.

Apples
○❖SPRING/AUTUMN

Apples will grow in containers as long as they are well fed and watered. It is important to choose a variety on a dwarfing rootstock so that it does not grow too big, and to stake it firmly (*see* pages 38–9). Most cultivars need cross-pollinating to produce fruit, so grow varieties with overlapping flowering periods.

Apricots, cherries, damsons, greengages, nectarines, peaches, plums
○❖SUMMER/AUTUMN

Fruit in the *Prunus* family can be grown in containers as long as dwarfing rootstocks are selected and they are given adequate water and food. They can be trained as fans or cordons and will thrive against a warm wall or fence.

Aubergines
○ ✿ ❖SUMMER

Small 'baby' aubergines – not much bigger than your finger or a golf ball and produced on dwarf plants – are ideal for growing in pots on a sheltered, sunny patio. Give the plants supports, such as bamboo canes, and keep them well watered: aubergines need high humidity.

Beans
○ ✿ ❖SUMMER

Dwarf varieties of both runner and French beans are suitable for growing in containers or growing bags. With their colourful flowers and long pods, they can be ornamental as well as delicious to eat. Start to harvest the beans as they reach about 10cm (4in) long, and pick regularly to ensure a continued supply and prevent them from becoming stringy.

Beetroot, Swiss chard
○❖SUMMER

Beetroot and Swiss chard may be grown for cropping or for their foliage. Beetroot (above) is naturally biennial, but it is grown as an annual and can be used fresh or pickled. It may be red, golden or white. Swiss chard is a close relative. Its leaves are edible, having similar uses to spinach, and the stalks are highly ornamental, so the plant can serve a dual function where space is limited, allowing you to enjoy the colours before you harvest your crop. Swiss chard can be harvested all winter when conditions permit.

Carrots
○❖SUMMER to AUTUMN/WINTER

Carrots are great for growing in containers, especially for children as there is an almost instant result. Many new introductions (labelled 'patio vegetables') mature quickly and produce small, sweet carrots that can be eaten raw. If you sow thickly, you can begin pulling baby carrots within weeks. You can experiment and grow white, orange and purple carrots; different-coloured vegetables contain different nutrients.

Citrus fruits
○ ❖YEAR-ROUND (under glass)

This group of evergreen plants includes oranges, lemons, limes, grapefruit and calamondins (above). Calamondins are a cross between a mandarin and a kumquat and are one of the best to grow in pots. Citrus fruits have glossy, dark-green foliage and small, fragrant, waxy white flowers in spring and summer. Unripe green fruits are often carried at the same time as ripe ones. Some are bitter but can be used in preserves.

Courgettes, cucumbers
○ ❖SUMMER

Courgettes (zucchini) are small cultivars of marrow, harvested when they are immature, while the skin is smooth and shiny. Fruit colours range from dark green through to yellow. Cucumbers need a frost-free environment with as much warmth and humidity as possible. To save space, train them vertically as a cordon with support strings twisted around the plants to hold them upright. The main stem is kept growing upwards and the sideshoots are trimmed back to two or three leaves.

Figs
○ ❖SUMMER to AUTUMN

Figs are among the oldest fruits in cultivation and they will crop well as long as they are in a warm, sheltered position. They thrive within the confines of a large container when they are well watered and fed, and can be fan-trained against a wall or fence. Protect the fruit from birds by draping the whole tree with netting.

Grapes
○ ❖SPRING/SUMMER/AUTUMN

Grapes are both attractive and versatile in a small garden, and may be ornamental (with green or purple foliage) or fruiting types. They can be trained over a sunny wall, a railing or a pergola, to provide shade. The fruit can be blackish purple, greenish white or yellow depending on the cultivar. If you have a hot, sunny growing area, it's worth considering a grape vine as new, more resilient varieties are being introduced that can withstand cold weather over winter. (Frost hardiness depends on variety.)

Lettuces
○ (some types) ❖SPRING to AUTUMN

You can have delicious outdoor lettuces on the table all year round, provided you use a number of different varieties. The main categories of lettuce are butterhead, loose-leaf and cos. All can be grown in containers as long as they are well fed and given sufficient water. Butterhead varieties are quick to mature, with soft, smooth leaves and a loose heart. Loose-leaf varieties do not form a heart as such, so leaves can be removed on a cut-and-come-again basis. Winter-hardy varieties are available but protect them from frost.

Peppers
○ ❖SUMMER

Peppers of all kinds can be grown quite easily in containers, although they need fairly high temperatures and humidity to fruit well. The fruits can be red, yellow, orange or bluish black, depending on the cultivar. The strength of flavour can range from mild bell peppers to very hot chillies, with strength increasing as the fruit ripens. Many are highly ornamental as they grow, so you can have an attractive plant as well as tasty fruit.

Potatoes
● ❄ (some types) ❖SPRING to AUTUMN

Potatoes come in a range of shapes, sizes, colours and textures. They may be round, oval or knobbly and the flesh white, cream, yellow or blue. They mature at different times, leading to classification as First Early, Second Early (or Mid-crop) or Maincrop. The first two are better for containers, as they mature more quickly and do not take up space for as long as Maincrop types. (Frost hardiness depends on variety.)

Radicchio
○ ❖AUTUMN

Radicchio (also known as red chicory) is grown like a lettuce, with a large heart for eating raw with salad: it can also be roasted or grilled. The flavour of the red leaves is distinctive and slightly bitter when uncooked. Pick the leaves as required, leaving the plant to continue growing, but take care not to over-harvest, which will leave the plant too weak to grow. Alternatively, cut the whole plant off just above the compost and leave the roots to sprout again.

Rocket
○ ❖SUMMER

This tender-looking plant is actually quite hardy and will survive most winters outdoors provided it has some shelter and does not get waterlogged. The leaves have a sharp, spicy flavour that increases in strength as the plant matures. It is a versatile vegetable that can be eaten raw in salads or cooked like spinach. It can be grown as individual plants or harvested regularly as a cut-and-come-again crop all season.

Strawberries
○ ❖SUMMER

These low-growing herbaceous plants (above, 'Pegasus') grow and crop well in containers. Many varieties produce all their fruit in a one-month period during the summer. To extend the cropping period, choose a mixture of varieties with different cropping times; or select a perpetual variety that will crop less heavily but continuously throughout the summer. Alpine varieties such as 'Mignonette' produce tiny, sweet fruits throughout summer and autumn.

Tomatoes
○ ✺ ❖SUMMER

Tomatoes are versatile and reliable plants that will grow in growing bags or pots, window boxes and hanging baskets (depending on the variety) and give a good yield in most years. They do need sunshine and warmth for ripening the fruit, so prefer a sheltered, sunny position. Some varieties, for instance 'Moneymaker', are best staked and grown as cordons (as a single stem with the sideshoots removed). Others, like the bush varieties (for example cherry and berry types) are best left to grow as bushes, without having the sideshoots removed. These types are particularly good for containers, as they're smaller and need less attention. All will need staking.

Don't forget

If you're using growing bags for tomatoes, you can get a second crop from the bag after harvesting by sowing or planting a quick crop such as lettuces or baby carrots once the tomatoes have been removed. There will be a residue of fertilizer in the bag if you have fed the tomatoes regularly, so the next crop won't even need feeding.

Herbs

One of the great things about having herbs in pots is that you can keep them by the door, picking leaves for cooking without trudging around in the rain or the dark. Some last all year, some are herbaceous, others are annual. Plan your herb garden with this in mind and you can make an attractive feature of it.

Basil
◑ ❀ ❖SUMMER

Basil is usually grown as a half-hardy annual (put outdoors after the danger of frost has passed) or a short-lived perennial (in frost-free areas). It needs a warm, sheltered position to grow well, as it is easily damaged by wind and scorched by direct sun. The aromatic, bright-green leaves are delicious in tomato sauces, pasta dishes, salads, vinegars and pesto.

Chives
○ ❖SUMMER

Alliums include shallots (*Allium cepa*), garlic (*A. sativum*) and chives (*A. schoenoprasum*). Chives are grown for their edible, hollow, dark-green leaves, which have a mild onion flavour. They produce round heads of purple or white flowers in summer. All alliums prefer a sunny spot with good drainage and plenty of food. The smaller forms are best for containers.

Dill
○ ❖SUMMER

Dill is an aniseed-scented biennial, more commonly grown as an annual. It has feathery, blue-green foliage on smooth, hollow stems, and flattened heads of yellow flowers in summer. Add chopped leaves (fresh or dried) to soups, eggs, salmon and potato salad; and the seed to fish dishes, pickles, apple pie, cakes and bread. It is inclined to bolt (flower prematurely) if it is not watered enough. Dill looks attractive where the feathery leaves grow up through lower plants and create a misty effect.

Bay
○ ◑ ❖SPRING

This makes an attractive tree or shrub as well as adding flavour to soups and casseroles. You can shape the plant into a pyramid, ball or standard (*see* pages 52–3). Give bay a sunny or partially shaded position. It dislikes cold winds, but is tolerant of heat.

Coriander
○ ❖SUMMER

Fresh coriander leaves add an authentic flavour to Asian and Middle Eastern dishes. Soil should be light and well-drained and the container placed in a sunny spot. Pick the leaves all summer as you need them and water regularly to stop the plant flowering too early.

Lemon balm
◑ ❖SUMMER

Lemon balm is a hardy herbaceous perennial with heavily aromatic, lemon-scented foliage. Fresh leaves can be applied directly to insect bites, used in a soothing infusion to ease tension and headaches, or added to sweet and savoury dishes as well as vinegars. They are also included in aromatic pillows and pot-pourri. This is an invasive plant, however, that can self-seed and become a nuisance if not watched!

Mint
○ ❖SUMMER

The mint family is large and includes a wide range of hardy, spreading, aromatic perennials. Growing them in containers is a good way to keep them under control, although they will need dividing and repotting regularly. Recommended forms include: *Mentha × gracilis* 'Variegata' (ginger mint); *M. × piperita* f. *citrata* (eau-de-Cologne mint); *M. requienii* (Corsican mint); *M. pulegium* (pennyroyal); *M. spicata* (spearmint); *M. suaveolens* 'Variegata' (pineapple mint, above).

Parsley
○ ◑ ❖SUMMER

Parsley is a hardy biennial, commonly grown as an annual. The edible, mid-green leaves are popular in cooking and as a garnish. There are two main types: *Petroselinum crispum* (above) has densely curled, moss-like leaves, carried on hollow stems; French or Italian parsley (*P.c.* var. *neapolitanum*) has flat leaves and a stronger flavour. Neither tolerates being left standing in waterlogged compost. Use the leaves in their first year, and trim regularly.

Sage
○ ◑ ❖SUMMER

This is a woody sub-shrub with aromatic, woolly, evergreen leaves on square stems (often with a reddish tinge). It produces lilac-blue flowers in summer, in spikes at the tips of the stems. As well as green-leaved forms, there are attractively variegated (*Salvia officinalis* 'Tricolor') and purple-leaved ('Purpurascens') varieties. Sage is a good-looking plant and it is also a useful ingredient. The leaves are often cooked with fatty meats, such as pork, to aid digestion.

Oregano
○ ❖SUMMER

This name covers oregano and marjoram, which are both hardy herbaceous perennials with aromatic, oval leaves. They will tolerate a hot, sunny position, preferring alkaline conditions. Gold-leaved forms need shade from hot midday sun. The leaves can be used fresh, dried or frozen. Clip the plants regularly to stop them from becoming long and straggly – you can dry the trimmed leaves and store them in airtight bottles for use later when there are fewer on the plant to pick fresh.

Rosemary
○ ❖SPRING to LATE SUMMER

Rosemary is a hardy shrub with narrow, aromatic, evergreen leaves that can be used fresh or dried to flavour hot and cold dishes. Small flowers are produced in spring and summer, in shades of purple-blue to mauve and white. Trim regularly to control straggling shoots and encourage bushing. These plants do not respond well to hard pruning and may even die. Like bay and sage, rosemary is a dual-purpose plant, being both attractive and useful.

Thyme
○ ◑ ❖MID- to LATE SUMMER

This is a small, shrubby perennial with thin, twiggy stems and small, oval, grey-green, fragrant leaves. *Thymus × citriodorus* (above) is lemon-scented. Clusters of tiny pale-lavender flowers, attractive to bees, appear from mid- to late summer on the tips of the shoots. Prune frequently to keep the plant dense and bushy. Grow in low pots close to pathways, so the aroma is released as people brush past the plants. The form 'Silver Queen' is cream-variegated.

Water plants

Some water plants are hardy; others may have to be replaced every year (especially if you live in a particularly cold area). Not all water plants are suitable for containers, as they can become invasive and will quickly choke out any other plants. So, before you buy, always find out whether the plant you like is suitable for the size and type of container you wish to plant.

Orontium aquaticum Golden club
○ ❖ SPRING to SUMMER

This is a marginal perennial that likes deep mud, or water no deeper than 45cm (18in), and spreads well. Its flowers are yellow, produced at the top of a club-shaped white spadix (hence its common name). Orontiums like the same conditions as irises; they grow well together if you divide both regularly.

Aponogeton distachyos
Water hawthorn
○ ❖ SPRING/AUTUMN

This vigorous, deep-water perennial remains evergreen in most winters. It has small, white, hawthorn-scented flowers with purple-black stamens. This plant is invasive, so you need only one or two in a container. Ensure the water is 30–90cm (12–36in) deep. The oval leaves float on the surface.

Mimulus luteus
Yellow monkey flower
○ ❖ LATE SPRING to SUMMER

This is a vigorous, spreading, marginal plant with lax stems, mid-green leaves and golden, trumpet-shaped flowers. Grow in soil at the edge of a container of water up to 7cm (3in) deep. The plant will eventually spill over the sides of the containerized pond.

Veronica beccabunga Brooklime
○ ❖ SPRING to LATE SUMMER

This pretty veronica has white-eyed blue flowers. It will live in water up to 10cm (4in) deep, making it a useful addition to a small patio water feature or the very edge of a larger one where, like *Mimulus*, it will spill over the edge and hide the sides. It is usually evergreen throughout the year.

Iris Water iris
○ ◑ ❖ EARLY to MIDSUMMER

Only *I. laevigata* (such as 'Rose Queen', above) and *I. ensata* (syn. *I. kaempferi*) are suitable for containers. They are hardy, rhizomatous plants with beardless purple, blue, pink, red, yellow or white flowers. Plant them at the margin of a containerized pond, preferably in partial shade.

Nymphaea Water lily
○ ❖ SUMMER

The queen of aquatic plants can be found in sizes small enough for a half-barrel or other container. The circular floating leaves are followed by sometimes scented flowers in white or shades of red, pink, orange and yellow. *N. tetragona* and *N.* 'Pygmaea Helvola' (above) are the tiniest water lilies, spreading to 25–40cm (10–16in) with flowers 2.5–5cm (1–2in) across.

Other water plants for containers

Butomus umbellatus Flowering rush
○ ❖ LATE SUMMER
Twisty leaves, delicate pink flowers.

Isolepis cernua Slender sedge
○ ❖ SUMMER
Small dense clump of fine stems, producing brown flower spikelets.

Containers season by season

Gardening tasks are seasonal, and yet the seasons are never as predictable (and 'on time') as we feel they ought to be. To make things more complicated, the climate changes from year to year, and from one region to another. This section therefore gives an overview of what should be done in each season (whenever the season arrives for you) rather than which jobs should be done in which month. The trick is to think in 'plant time'. The most successful gardeners are the ones who keep a close eye on the weather!

Spring

Spring is the busiest time in the garden, as everything bursts into life and the plants for the coming season all demand attention at once. Sometimes it's hard to find time for all the jobs that are waiting, but it's all worth it as your seedlings and young plants start to grow, established plants begin to put out new growth and all the bulbs you planted last autumn burst into full colour. Winter is behind you now and the whole season lies ahead, so take time out to enjoy the lengthening days and warmer temperatures.

If you don't have the patience or time to raise plants from seed, plug plants are ideal. As soon as you get them, pot them up individually into 9cm (3in) compost-filled pots.

Young and plug plants

Plug plants are so called because they are rooted into a tiny plug of compost in a cell tray, which is easy to transport and send by post. If you have mail-ordered young or plug plants, open them up as soon as they arrive – to allow light and air to reach them – and water them immediately. Pot them up into small pots filled with seed or potting compost as soon as you can.

These young plants have been grown in warm nursery conditions, so make sure you keep them under cover with full protection from frost. You may need to shade the sensitive leaves from bright sun at this stage, so they don't scorch. Lay a piece of horticultural fleece over the top of new leaves or apply shading paint to the outside of the greenhouse. If the leaves are particularly limp or the plants are at all dried out, cover them with a propagator lid or white plastic bag (held in place with an elastic band) for a few days while they recover. This will keep the humidity high and reduce the stress of losing water through the leaves. Pot them on into slightly larger pots when they are growing strongly and their roots have filled the first pot.

Seed and seedlings

Spring is a busy time for sowing seed and looking after young seedlings, but you need to be on your guard. A random hot day or cold night can be fatal to these tender little plants and you could easily lose a whole batch. Make sure you remove any covering that you laid over the seed as soon as the seedlings begin to emerge, although you can leave a raised cover (such as a propagator lid) in place. Once the seedlings are growing well, take the cover off completely during the day to allow air to circulate, as this reduces the chance of fungal infection taking hold. Replace it at night, together with layers of protective horticultural fleece for insulation.

Some of the early vegetables will be growing already, but you can sow lettuce, rocket and spinach to harvest for salads, along with radishes and spring onions, to harvest in about 8 to 12 weeks' time. Also, sow early carrots and peas, tomatoes, chillies, sweet peppers, aubergines and beans (runner, French and broad) for harvesting in summer (*see* pages 96–8). Now is also the time to start sowing a succession of herbs to crop throughout spring and summer (*see* pages 99–100).

For flowering containers, begin sowing hardy and half-hardy annuals (*see* pages 91–5) towards the end of spring (*see* pages 60–1). Your sweet pea seedlings should be growing well by now and should have been pinched out at the tops to make them branch.

Pricking out and hardening off

Once the seedlings are large enough to handle (or are developing their first set of 'true' leaves), they can be

About two or three weeks before your last expected frost, move young and tender plants out of the greenhouse during the day and bring them in at night. After this, they should be ready to plant out.

Planting and potting

Pot up dormant bulbs such as lilies, begonias, cannas and dahlias (*see* pages 88–92). This will give them time to start into growth, ready for transplanting to their final seasonal container for the summer.

Divide pots of perennial herbs such as chives and mint that you used last year. Repot the best of the removed material in fresh compost and discard any damaged or shrivelled roots. You can plant up a herb hanging basket to keep by the kitchen door so you can reach the herbs without going outside when cooking (*see* pages 99–100).

'Chit' seed potatoes by standing them in an egg box for two or three weeks so that the new shoots begin to develop. Once they have several new shoots, you can pot them up.

moved into individual pots (*see* page 61). Always hold them by a leaf, rather than by the stem, because if you damage a leaf the plant can grow another, but if you damage the stem the plant will die.

There can be a big difference between the conditions where you raised your young plants and the great outdoors. If you transfer the plants too quickly from one to the other, the shock may harm them, so get them used to it gradually. This is what is meant by 'hardening off'. Towards the end of the season, put them outside during the day as long as the conditions are calm (and not too wet). You'll still need to move them under cover at night. After two or three weeks' hardening off, it should be safe to leave them out, but keep an eye on the weather.

It's lovely to be able to enjoy fresh salads in spring, particularly if they're home grown. Even if you don't have a garden, you can still create your own mini veg and herb patch in a hanging basket by the back door.

At this time of year, you may be running a bit short of containers. With potatoes, there is a very effective alternative in that they will grow perfectly well in bags (bin liners or compost bags with drainage holes pierced in them). (*See also* page 98.)

Plant young strawberries (*see* page 98 and right) in hanging baskets or other suitable containers to get them off to an early start.

As tomato plants (*see* page 98) get bigger, plant them into pots or growing bags and remove any sideshoots that develop on cordon (single-stem) types (*see* box, below right). Leave bush types unchecked. Put them outdoors when danger of frost is passed – usually late May. Expect outdoor tomatoes to start ripening in midsummer; they'll continue until cold autumn weather stops further growth and the plants are killed by frost. Pick any remaining green fruits for ripening indoors or making chutney.

Freshen winter pots

The containers you planted and put outside last autumn to give colour through the winter will be starting to look jaded by now. If you feel they need jazzing up but don't want to create a new display from scratch straight away, you can freshen up large containers quite easily by plunging new pots of spring bulbs or bedding plants such as pansies or primulas into the compost between the 'old' plants. This will help keep a fresh display that changes regularly and never gets time to look tired, and is a quick way to liven up the container if you're expecting visitors!

Strawberries grow surprisingly well in hanging baskets. Place about five plants around the edge of the basket and pinch out any runners that form. By the second year you'll have an abundance of luscious red fruit.

Spring is the time to pot up dormant bulbs such as lilies (shown here), begonias, cannas and dahlias. These will all provide a lovely display in summer. Most look best planted in individual groups.

HOW TO grow tomatoes in pots

Transplant young tomato plants to larger pots of fresh compost. Push a cane in behind the plant, 5cm (2in) away from the stem, and tie the plant loosely to the cane with soft garden twine. Water the plants in, and place them in a sunny, sheltered spot. Give a diluted liquid feed once or twice a week, wetting the compost thoroughly. As the plants grow, keep tying the stem to the cane.

Train upright varieties as a single stem by pinching out any sideshoots that develop. Take care not to break off the flower trusses. Nip the growing tips out after three or four trusses of fruit have formed, to encourage the remaining ones to ripen. Bush cultivars don't need trimming or training, but use several canes to support the stems, so they don't break under the weight of the fruit.

You'll be bringing half-hardy or tender plants such as pelargoniums out of the greenhouse towards the end of spring, once danger of frost has passed. Pick off dead leaves to prevent possible disease.

If you want to ring the changes, you can completely replant your winter containers with fresh spring bedding plants, such as pansies, primroses, polyanthus and double daisies, and with flowering bulbs such as daffodils, tulips, grape hyacinths and crocuses.

The previous plants are unlikely to have rooted deeply over the winter months so, to save money and resources, leave the lower part of the old compost in the pot and simply replace the top layer around the new plants with fresh.

Maintaining existing containers

Pick over shrubs and perennials to remove dead leaves, old stems and any other accumulated debris.

Trim off any woody stems that have been damaged or have died back over the winter. Prune late-flowering shrubs and climbers, to prompt them into growth, as well as early-flowering shrubs after the flowers die off (see pages 50–2). Check stakes and supports and tie plants in if they have come loose.

Apply a general fertilizer to every pot (see pages 48–9 and below). Early spring is the time to start watering larger containers regularly (see pages 46–7), because the leaf canopy may shade the compost from rain. If some plants, such as camellias, dry out now, they will shed their flower buds unopened.

Remove the faded flowerheads from spring-flowering bulbs to save them wasting energy producing seed, and give them a feed with a high-potash fertilizer as they die down. Allow the leaves to die down completely before removing them so that the energy goes back into the base of the bulb.

The flush of spring growth makes plants grow very rapidly, so this is the time when they are most likely to need repotting (see pages 44–5). The exceptions are plants that flower now, because any disturbance at this stage might make them abort their flower buds and you will lose the whole display for this year.

If you have a water feature (see pages 40–3), remove winter debris such as dead leaves, and clean the various parts, including the pump filter, before topping up the reservoir ready for the season. If you have plants in the feature, they may need lifting and dividing, and they'll certainly need feeding with an aquatic fertilizer to help them grow through the coming season.

Towards the end of spring, you'll need to start feeding your container plants regularly. Use liquid or soluble feed and dilute it according to the manufacturer's instructions. Also, use slow-release fertilizer when planting.

Daffodils and other spring-flowering bulbs should be dead-headed regularly. Remove the flowerhead but leave the stalk; nutrients in the stem will be transported back to the bulb to produce flowers next year.

Stars of spring

These plants look stunning on their own or you can use them in combination for a spectacular display. For a large container, plant a small conifer or other structural plant to form the framework, add small, hardy evergreens, such as heathers, and then use the flowers below to fill the gaps with colour. A trailing plant, such as a small-leaved ivy, will flow over the edges of the pot to soften the effect.

BULBS
Convallaria (lily-of-the-valley)
Crocus
Fritillaria (fritillaries)
Galanthus (snowdrops)
Hyacinthus (hyacinths)
Muscari (grape hyacinths)
Narcissus (daffodils)
Tulipa (tulips)

ANNUAL BEDDING PLANTS
Bellis perennis (daisy)
Erysimum cheiri cultivars (wallflowers, dwarf types)
Matthiola (stocks, dwarf types)
Myosotis (forget-me-nots)
Ornamental cabbages
Primula (includes primrose and polyanthus)
Viola (pansies)

Be prepared

■ Slugs, snails, woodlice and early aphids are all very hungry at this time of year, and the tender young shoots on established plants are perfect for them, as are emerging seedlings. Woodlice usually live on decaying wood, but the moisture in a seedling is enough to tempt them in spring and they will go for the roots. Be ready with your preferred means of control, so that you can deal with them before the population becomes large enough to present a problem (*see* pages 56–8).

■ Be on your guard for frost, which can ruin all your early efforts. Some areas, such as the coast, seldom have to worry about late frost, but everyone else needs to be wary until the end of spring. Have some horticultural fleece, bubble wrap or newspaper handy (*see* page 55). Remember not to leave bubble wrap over or around the plants during the day, because it can damage them.

■ Strong winds at this time of year can damage soft new shoots, particularly on climbers if you haven't tied them to the support. Taller plants may blow over, so make sure they're well watered to increase the weight and wedge other pots around them to stop them moving.

■ Excessive rain can cause waterlogging if the drainage hole in the container is blocked or if the pot is standing on the ground and the water is slow to drain. To avoid this, raise the container up on pot feet. If the pot becomes waterlogged, lie it on its side for a day to let the excess water drain out.

■ Hot sun can catch you out in spring, because you may not be expecting it to be quite as hot as it is, particularly through glass. It only takes a brief period of intense sun on the tender leaves of seedlings to scorch them beyond repair. Protect seedlings from hot, direct sun with netting or greenhouse shading.

A blaze of colour is just what's needed to raise spirits in spring, after a cold, bleak winter. Tulips are arguably the most opulent spring flowers, ranging from soft pastels to rich, sumptuous colours.

Summer

This is when the garden comes into its own: suddenly you realize that all the hard work is paying off. It's not all rest though: you need to keep everything in tip-top condition with a regular routine of watering, feeding and dead-heading to keep the display looking its best for as long as possible. If you didn't plant up your pots and hanging baskets in spring, there is still a chance to do so in early summer.

By midsummer, most shrubs have finished flowering. However, pots of annuals and tender perennials will extend the season, providing colourful flowers into early autumn.

Feeding

Summer is a time of very active growth, so feed all permanent plants once a month throughout summer (*see* pages 48–9), to keep them healthy, and to help them fight off

Watering is one of the major jobs in summer, and you frequently have to water containers once, sometimes twice a day. Use water-retaining crystals when planting to reduce the amount of watering necessary.

pest or disease attack (*see* pages 56–9) and cope with heat and dry conditions. Bedding and fast-growing vegetables will need a boost every week. Continue to feed any spring bulbs that are still dying down, as this will improve flowering next year.

Protecting plants from heat and water loss

The intense sun during the summer months can quickly scorch leaves or plants that prefer a modicum of shade. Checking for water requirements regularly will reduce the likelihood of scorch (*see* pages 46–7). Water thoroughly onto the compost when necessary. Outdoor plants that suffer in intense sun may need to be tucked behind a more tolerant neighbour or moved to a shady spot before they begin to suffer. If you have a greenhouse or conservatory, make sure you provide some form of shade. This may consist of shading paint over the

outside, blinds or roller screens attached inside or out, or fleece held up with clips or on canes inside.

Plants lose water through their leaves all the time, but you can reduce the loss if you keep the air around the plants moist and humid. Damp down the floor of your greenhouse, conservatory, balcony or patio to increase evaporation around the plants and raise humidity levels. In a hot greenhouse or conservatory, you can stand leafy plants on a saucer of pebbles or gravel that you keep topped up with water. The plant itself should never sit in the water, which may rot the roots, but the water can evaporate up around the leaves and keep the humidity high in the immediate vicinity. Humidity also keeps several pests at bay, including red spider mite (*see* pages 56–8).

It's one of life's ironies that most people go on holiday when the weather is at its warmest and the garden is looking lovely. Plants in pots are more susceptible to drought than anything else in the garden. Ideally, you'll get a gardening friend to water your plants for you, but failing that here are some tips for helping them to survive while you're away.

■ If you're often away for a few days at a time or more, it's well worth investing in a watering system that connects to the mains and delivers water to each pot. You can fit an automatic timer to the system (*see* pages 46–7.)

■ A home-made alternative, which will last a few days, is to make a reservoir out of an old plastic drinks bottle with a screw cap. Make a hole in the base, loosen the cap and sink the bottle into the compost upside down with the new hole uppermost. Fill the bottle through this hole. The water should seep out gradually through the thread of the cap.

■ Move all containers out of direct sunlight and position them closer together to reduce moisture loss. When plants are grouped together, the leaves form layers that trap moisture underneath and create a microclimate with higher humidity.

■ Stand the plants in saucers of gravel filled with water. This allows evaporation around the leaves and the compost will be able to suck water out of the saucer. Don't leave the plant sitting in water like this for longer than a week or two, as the roots could rot.

Young plants

Check all cuttings for signs of rooting. Once they begin to grow, pot them separately. They will still need protection until they're used to supporting themselves. Make sure you keep pests away, water them regularly and shade them from hot sun (*see* opposite). This is the time to start sowing biennial plants for next year, because they will grow in their first year and flower in the second.

Climbers

Tie in the new growth of all climbers as it gets longer, before it can damage itself by rubbing against other shoots or blowing in the wind. Early-flowering forms of clematis that have already flowered can be pruned now to keep the growth under control. Remove the seedheads from early-flowering climbers to save the plant wasting energy on seed you don't need. If you do require seed, leave a limited number of seedheads to develop. The fewer there are, the better quality the seed will be. Climbing roses need regular checking for signs of pests and diseases in summer (*see* pages 56–9).

Flowers

Spring bulbs that have died down can be lifted for storage in a cool, dry, shaded place over summer. You can reclaim the containers to use again. Summer bulbs should be growing well and starting to flower.

Taller flowers need staking before the weight of the flowers pulls the stem over, especially after heavy rain. Stake perennials as they grow so that the new foliage hides the support (*see* pages 38–9).

If you want to save seed, cut off whole seedheads in summer or early autumn as they turn brown but before they're completely ripe and start to shed. Place the seed in a labelled paper bag for storage. (*See also* pages 112–13.)

Vegetables and fruit

Make sure you keep all your edible plants well watered at all times. Keep sowing successive batches of salad leaves, and herbs such as basil, to be

When growing ornamental climbers up a support such as a trellis or wigwam, tie in the new growth as it extends, using garden twine or special garden ties. Attach it loosely to avoid damaging the stems.

Place seed collected from semi-ripe seedheads in a brown paper bag secured with string and hang the bags in a warmish place until dry. Never use polythene bags because they're likely to cause rot.

harvested fresh throughout summer. You should also be harvesting peas, mangetout, beans, aubergines, potatoes, tomatoes, raspberries and stone fruit.

Continue to remove the sideshoots from cordon tomatoes (*see* page 105), and pinch out the growing tips after four or five trusses of fruit have formed to encourage ripening.

Protect ripening strawberries from pests and rain damage. If you want to increase your stock of strawberries, allow the plants to grow runners, then peg these down into small pots of seed compost using thin wire bent into the shape of a hairpin. Once the runners have developed their own root system, detach them from the parent plant and grow them on ready for next year.

Watch out for various pests as well as diseases such as rust and powdery mildew (see pages 56–9).

Summer displays can be wonderfully hot and fiery. Here, bright orange and red begonias vie for attention while the lilies and white galtonia bells provide a restful contrast.

Runner beans are the perfect plant for the novice veg gardener. They grow happily in pots on a patio, they're highly ornamental and yield a mass of beans for summer meals.

Stars of summer

There's a wider choice of flowering plants available in summer than at any other time of year. You may choose to fill your containers with annual bedding so you can ring the changes every year, or use perennials that will carry on year after year. Fewer bulbs are flowering now, but the lilies and alliums are varied enough to make up for that. Summer bedding is diverse, colourful and wonderful value for money, as long as you keep it watered, fed and healthy. It's also easy to add to your permanent containers, if there's room, to liven them up for the summer months.

BULBS
Agapanthus campanulatus
Allium cristophii
Lilium (lilies)

SHRUBS
Cistus (sun roses)
Convolvulus cneorum
Santolina chamaecyparissus
Senecio

PERENNIALS
Echinops ritro (globe thistle)
Iris germanica hybrids
Kniphofia (red-hot poker)
Monarda (bergamot)
Verbascum (mullein)

BEDDING PLANTS
Argyranthemum
Begonia
Canna
Dahlia
Gazania
Helianthus annuus (sunflower)
Impatiens (busy lizzies)
Lathyrus odoratus (sweet pea)
Leucanthemum
Lobelia
Nemesia
Nicotiana (tobacco plants)
Papaver (poppies)
Pelargonium
Petunia
Tagetes (marigolds)
Verbena
Zinnia

Autumn

As the days shorten, plant growth begins to slow down, so this is the time to make the most of the plants that are still in colour and to begin preparing for the following year. It's time to stop dead-heading and let seedheads develop. Bulbs can be planted for next spring, or they can be forced for the winter months so you have some colour indoors. Autumn is the season for clearing up and preparing the containers for the winter, so make sure you have some horticultural fleece and sheets of bubble wrap for the cold nights that are coming soon.

Plant bulbs

This is the time to plant spring bulbs (*see* page 37) and the shops will be full of tempting varieties. The earlier you can buy and plant yours, the better, because the bulbs will be fresher and healthier and they will have the maximum time to establish before the cold weather sets in. The only danger with early planting is a late warm spell that can trick the bulbs into producing too much growth at the expense of the flowers. You can minimize the effect of this by standing the pot in a shady spot for the first few weeks and putting a topping over the compost after planting (*see* page 30).

Permanent containers

Keep watering pots if the weather is dry, although the need for water will be reducing now. Stop feeding permanent plants until spring. Remove dead flowerheads, dead stems, old foliage and fallen leaves before they get soggy and smother the plant underneath. Tidy up and divide large, fibrous-rooted perennials, keeping the healthy growth and discarding the rest. Mulch the surface of compost to give the roots some protection.

Autumn is the time to prepare for cold and windy weather. Towards the end of the season, protect plants by grouping the containers and moving them closer to the wall. This helps to keep wind and rain off the plants and provides more warmth. Well before the first frost, lag outdoor tubs by wrapping newspaper or bubble wrap around the base (*see* page 55).

Plant rockery bulbs such as dwarf irises, fritillaries and ipheions in pots using a gritty, free-draining bulb potting compost. Overwinter in a cool, dry place and put pots out when the plants flower in spring.

Hyacinths for Christmas

Autumn is the time to plant hyacinths for Christmas flowering indoors. Look for the bulbs that are described as 'specially prepared for Christmas', as this means they have been given a heat treatment to get them ready for early flowering.

Plant each bulb in its own 10cm (4in) pot of bulb or multipurpose compost, with the nose of the bulb just above the surface. Water lightly to settle the compost and stand the pot in a cool, dark, frost-free place such as a shed or garage. Check regularly and water if the bulbs look dry: the compost should feel damp to the touch at all times. If a bulb is pushing itself right out of the compost, you may need to repot it. Hyacinths have very strong roots and if a bulb is planted too close to the surface, the roots will push it right up, usually at an angle. This leads to lopsided growth, a distorted flower and, normally, a wasted bulb.

When the leaves are about 5cm (2in) high, after about ten weeks, move the bulbs into a cool room in the house until the flower buds are showing. Select three or five bulbs at the same stage and replant them into a decorative bowl.

You can move the bowl into a warmer room as the flowers develop, so you can enjoy the fragrance, although they will last longer in a cool spot. As the flowers grow, they may need some support – sturdy garden twigs will do fine.

Autumn is a busy time in the vegetable garden as there's a lot to harvest at this time, including runner and French beans, marrows, courgettes, sweetcorn, lettuces, rocket, spring onions and cabbages.

Seasonal displays

Replace summer patio plants with winter and spring bedding plants in early and mid-autumn. Well before there's a risk of frost, pot up any tender perennials, such as pelargoniums and half-hardy fuchsias, and take them indoors or into the greenhouse over winter. Also, lift and store any summer-flowering bulbs.

Vegetables and fruit

Sow a last quick crop of leaves such as spinach and sow winter lettuce, overwintering spring onions, early carrots and mangetout (if you can provide protection from the cold). There will also be plenty of veg to harvest at this time (*see* pages 96–8). Leave the last of the tomatoes on the plants until the weather turns cold, then bring fruit indoors and store in a drawer or cupboard. If they're slow to turn red, put a ripe banana in with them. It will give off the 'ripening gas' ethylene, which should hasten things along. Pick the last of the raspberries, apples and pears. Store only perfect, healthy fruit and wrap each individually so that if there is a problem with one, it will be isolated from the rest.

Growing bags

There is still a lot of goodness left in a growing bag that has had tomatoes in, especially if you've fed them regularly. After removing the tomatoes, make the most of the nutritious compost by sowing a quick crop of salad leaves in the bag, either now or in spring.

Alternatively, use the old compost on the garden around your shrubs. The birds will quickly eat any insects that might have been in the bag.

To make herb-infused oils, place a few healthy, clean sprigs of herbs such as tarragon, thyme, rosemary or oregano in a bottle, cover with good-quality olive oil and leave for a few weeks in a cool cupboard.

In the greenhouse

Reduce watering and feeding in the greenhouse in autumn. As cropping plants finish, fill the space with tender plants that need protection. Plant herbs in containers for winter use, for example thyme, mint, parsley, oregano and basil. You can preserve leaves and stems now by drying or freezing them, or bottling them in oil. Pot up any remaining rooted cuttings. Cuttings that have not rooted by now are unlikely to do so and should be discarded before they rot.

Seed and seedheads

Leave seedheads on plants in autumn – they look attractive over winter, provide food for the birds and you can harvest them the following year. If you want to collect seed from your plants or use seedheads for indoor decoration, hang the seedheads upside down in a dark, airy place to dry. To prevent losing the seed, either tie a paper bag over the seedhead before it opens so all the seeds are trapped inside the bag (*see* page 109), or place a piece of newspaper underneath to catch the seeds as they fall. Alternatively, lay the plant in a seed tray lined with newspaper. Some seed capsules 'explode' as they release the seed; where this is the case, you'll need to use the paper bag method, or you'll never find the seed again. Sort through

Don't forget

Watch out for late activity of vine weevils, snails, slugs and mice, particularly if the weather is mild. Also, beware of frost and heavy rain, which can damage container plants very quickly at this time.

You can collect and store seed from plants you already have in your garden. Wait until the seedpods turn brown, then shake the seeds out of each pod and store in a cool, dry place until ready to sow.

the debris and remove any bits of stem, leaf or seedpod.

Seed begins to deteriorate quickly if it's not kept in the right conditions. It's vital to keep it as dry as possible, because moisture encourages fungal mould or rotting and the seed is less likely to germinate. Once you've harvested the seed, store it in a clearly labelled paper envelope inside a clean glass jar, preferably made of brown glass, with a screw-top lid. Seal tightly and place the jar in a dark, cool but frost-free spot until you need it. The salad drawer of the fridge is ideal.

There are still plenty of container plants that look fabulous in autumn – bamboos, grasses and autumn flowers such as the coppery spikes of *Agastache* 'Firebird', seen here.

Everlasting flowers such as statice, helichrysum and gypsophila can be dried to use in arrangements all year round. Remove the leaves and hang the flowers upside down, in bunches, in a dark, airy place such as a shed.

Stars of autumn

Autumn containers need filling with hardy plants that are able to withstand the chilly temperatures as we head into winter, but that doesn't mean that you can't have flowers. In early autumn there are still a lot of flowers lingering on from the summer, including dahlias, lilies and nerines; there are also many plants that will flower throughout the cold months: some even offer the bonus that they change the colour of their leaves after a frost. A few have brightly coloured berries for interest (*Gaultheria mucronata*), and many of the bedding plants listed below will flower from autumn through to spring.

HARDY EVERGREENS
Berberis darwinii
Buxus sempervirens (box)
Calluna vulgaris cultivars (heathers)
Choisya ternata (Mexican orange blossom)
Erica (heaths)
Euonymus fortunei
Gaultheria mucronata

EVERGREENS FOR SHELTERED SITES
Acacia dealbata (wattle)
Callistemon citrinus (crimson bottlebrush)
Clianthus puniceus (lobster claw)
Hebe

AUTUMN BEDDING
Argyranthemum
Bellis perennis (daisy)
Primula
Salvia lyrata
Tagetes (marigolds)
Verbena × *hybrida*
Viola (pansies)

BULBS
Agapanthus campanulatus
Allium
Amaryllis belladonna
Canna
Colchicum (autumn crocus)
Crocus speciosus
Cyclamen hederifolium
Dahlia
Iris reticulata
Lilium (lily)
Nerine bowdenii

Winter

While there's less happening in terms of planting and growing in the garden, winter is a good time to catch up on the routine jobs that will make next year easier. It's also the time to sit down and make plans for any changes you may want to make to the garden. Textured bark, coloured stems and a skeleton framework of twigs and tree trunks dominate the garden now; combine these with handsome evergreens and flowering plants in strategically placed containers and you'll wonder why you ever considered winter a 'dead' time of year.

Cleaning

Good hygiene can save your plants or containers from passing on pests and diseases from one season to the next. Put the pots and seed trays you intend to use for the forthcoming season into a bucket of disinfectant and give them a good scrub with a stiff brush to remove all traces of old compost, mould or

At the end of the season, give all your pots a really good soak and scrub in warm, soapy water. This will eliminate fungal spores and prevent the spread of pests and diseases. Store them indoors over winter.

algae. Fungal spores lurk in this old material, waiting for conditions to improve so they can grow again. You also need to scrub down the area you use for your seedlings and young plants if it's outdoors, because the spores (along with small pests) will hide in cracks in walls, fences and the ground. Stack the clean pots somewhere out of the weather ready to use in the spring.

Rake up and clear away the last of the leaves and debris. If they're left lying around, they can harbour pests and diseases as well as making a soggy mess that will exclude the light from the plant underneath. Dead-head winter-flowering bedding plants so the old flowers don't get a chance to rot or go mouldy. It also saves them wasting energy on producing unwanted seed and keeps them flowering for longer.

Outdoor containers

More plants are killed in winter by having frozen roots than by any other single cause. Use horticultural fleece, bubble wrap and newspaper to protect your containers from the winter cold (*see* page 55). Bubble wrap can protect

If you're planning to heat the greenhouse over winter, or just want to provide more insulation, line the roof with bubble wrap to reduce heat loss. Leave the ventilators free to provide fresh air on warm days.

the container and roots from several degrees of frost, but don't place it over the plant because the plastic will trap in the moisture that the plants give off. This will chill overnight and can freeze the leaves to the plastic, causing considerable damage. Use fleece or even an old net curtain over the plant, as they are 'breathable' materials and allow light and air to reach the plant.

Check containers regularly for watering and waterlogging. Even if the weather is chilly, the plants will still need some water to stay alive, so you may need to give them a water now and again. Conversely, if they get too wet, the roots can rot. Make sure the pots have good drainage and stand them up on bricks or pot feet to speed it up.

If the compost is really waterlogged, lie the pot on its side for a day to allow the excess water to drain out.

While most of the climbers are dormant, you can undo their fastenings and flop them forwards to allow access to their supports or trellis. This will enable you to make necessary repairs or apply a preservative treatment to the trellis ready for next season (make sure the preservative is plant friendly). Check also that the support is still securely anchored in place and cannot break loose in the wind. Once everything is in good working order, simply tie the plant stems back in place.

As long as there is no frost forecast overnight, this is a good time to prune plants such as grapevine, wisteria and late-flowering clematis. Tie the remaining growth to the support structure to form a framework for next year. Prune winter-flowering shrubs immediately after the flowers fade so that they have the maximum time to produce new shoots that will flower next year.

Under cover

Watering should be kept to a minimum now, because plants are slightly more tolerant of cold if they're on the dry side. Keep the compost barely moist.

Sow sweet peas, hardy bedding and early vegetables for next year, begin to chit the earliest potatoes (*see* page 104) and continue to take hardwood cuttings (*see* page 64).

(*see* page 104) ... (*see* page 64).

Don't forget

Check plants for early slug damage as well as for signs of aphids and vine weevil.

Protecting wall plants

To protect a wall shrub or climber from frost, fasten a wooden batten to the wall above the climber and screw two large cup hooks into it. Take a piece of horticultural fleece that is large enough to cover the plant right down to the ground. Turn one end over twice and staple it so there is a hem about 5cm (2in) deep, then repeat at the other end. Push a long cane inside the top hem and set it inside the hooks, then roll the fleece down over the plant. Push a second cane into the lower hem to weigh the fleece down and keep it in place.

In winter, architectural plants such as sculptural grasses or sedges (here, *Carex comans* 'Bronze Form') come into their own and can make a strong, dramatic focal point. This arrangement could be scaled down to make a striking, formal feature in a small garden.

Stars of winter

If you think that nothing much happens outdoors in winter, have another look: a great many plants flower at this time, and others have fabulous stem colour, leaves or fruit. And since there are considerably fewer pollinating insects around, plants have to work harder to attract their attention, which means that many winter-flowering shrubs are much more fragrant than their summer counterparts.

BULBS
Anemone blanda
Crocus
Eranthis hyemalis (winter aconite)
Galanthus nivalis (common snowdrop)
Narcissus (daffodil)

BEDDING PLANTS
Bellis perennis (daisy)
Erysimum cheiri cultivars (wallflowers)
Primula (primrose and polyanthus)
Viola (pansies)

PERENNIALS
Bergenia
Helleborus (hellebores)

CLIMBERS
Clematis armandii
Jasminum nudiflorum (winter jasmine)

SHRUBS AND TREES
Acer negundo (box elder)
Betula (birch)
Calluna vulgaris cultivars (heathers)
Corylus avellana 'Contorta' (contorted hazel)
Erica (heaths)
Garrya elliptica 'James Roof' (silk-tassel bush)
Prunus × *subhirtella* 'Autumnalis Rosea' (rosebud cherry)
Rosa rugosa (hedgehog rose)
Skimmia japonica

SHRUBS FOR WINTER FRAGRANCE
Chimonanthus praecox (wintersweet)
Clematis cirrhosa var. *balearica*
Lonicera fragrantissima (honeysuckle)
Mahonia × *media* 'Charity'
Sarcococca confusa (Christmas box)
Viburnum × *bodnantense* 'Dawn'
Viburnum tinus

Containers for challenging sites

Container gardening makes it possible to grow plants just about anywhere. But if the only spot you have for your containers is in dense shade, or – conversely – baking hot, it can be a bit of a challenge. On a balcony or roof, you may be waging war against the wind. In urban gardens, some plants fail to thrive because of pollution; near the coast, they have to combat salty winds. Gardening in such situations may seem daunting, but don't lose heart. There's a good selection of plants for every situation: select the right ones for the right spot and you'll enjoy success wherever you garden.

Windy sites

Whether you live in a built-up area or a rural spot on the coast, a very windy site can present a few problems. Wind gusting strongly around a building can make unstable containers topple, it may damage stems and leaves, and the plants will dry out more quickly than they would in a sheltered spot.

Particularly in its early days, the leaves of a plant are easily damaged by wind. They may develop brown edges or actually rip apart. During this time, it may be beneficial to erect a piece of hessian or windbreak material temporarily to protect the plant while it establishes. Once it's growing strongly, it will be able to cope with small amounts of damage and recover as long as you keep it well fed and watered. If the plant continues to suffer damage, then perhaps it's not the right plant for that position or maybe you'll have to consider installing a permanent windbreak.

Windbreaks and screens

Erecting a windbreak can help protect an area against wind, but make sure it's woven and porous rather than a solid barrier – a solid wall creates increased turbulence behind it that can do more damage than the wind itself. A woven windbreak is useful because you can usually see out, so you don't feel quite so enclosed, but it's usually difficult to see in, particularly if you grow plants against it. If you erect the windbreak before planting, you can begin to disguise it straight away; for instance, you could conceal black windbreak netting behind a trellis that you then cover with an attractive climbing plant.

It should be possible to find a windbreak that will fit in with your design, but you may have to be creative. Rolls of bamboo can be nailed to a frame (to hold them upright) to go with a tropical or Oriental design (see page 12). If you live by the coast, sail canvas will give a nautical theme, but large sheets will offer too much wind resistance. A small-scale wooden pergola with a vine growing over it or white-painted trellis would work in a Mediterranean setting (see page 13). Hessian, either plain or painted, is also very effective when nailed to a wooden frame, although it will need replacing every few years. Contemporary themes (see page 21) are harder to predict, because they vary according to fashion, but you can do a lot with paint.

You may not want a high screen all the way round an area or there may be just one aspect you most want to screen off. In this case, you can use a single tall specimen plant or a 'hedge-in-a-box' to block off that one view. You can also plant to conceal an unsightly view, such as a car park or nearby building.

Staking and tying in

Staking and tying in plants are more important in a windy area than in any other, because a loose stem can whip around in the wind and damage not

A trellis placed along the top of a garden wall and planted with climbers provides shelter from wind as well as privacy. Container plants can be particularly vulnerable to wind as they can topple over.

just itself, but other stems near by. During the growing season of spring and early summer, you'll need to check every three or four weeks that the ties are adequate, secure and not cutting into the stems.

Use sturdy supports, so that the plants' roots are held firmly, rather than just thin bamboo canes, which can flex in the wind. 'Wind rock' can make the plant literally rock backwards and forwards, breaking the roots that are holding the plant in place. A smaller root system makes the plant even more unstable, as well as causing it to dry out more quickly, and the broken roots can become potential entry sites for diseases. Frames and stakes that are anchored deeply into the compost are more secure than single thin canes (see pages 38–9).

Coastal situations

A coastal situation may have the advantage that it's frost-free, but the exposure brings its own set of conditions that need to be overcome. The winds at the coast are not just strong, they're likely to be salt-laden, so thin or tender leaves will be ruined.

In selecting plants for a windy site, look for adaptations that will help the plant survive the salt-laden winds. Plants with tough, waxy foliage (*Aucuba japonica*, *Griselinia littoralis* and *Hebe*), small leaves (*Escallonia*, *Olearia × haastii* and *Osmanthus*), grey or silver leaves (*Eryngium*, *Helichrysum italicum* and *Santolina chamaecyparissus*) and those with tough, strap-like foliage (*Cordyline* and *Phormium*) or rough-textured leaves (*Rosa rugosa*) all tend to be fairly resilient, as are small, low-growing perennials such as *Sedum*, *Geranium* or *Sempervivum*.

Some of these plants, such as the sea holly (*Eryngium*), would naturally occur in poor soil near a beach, where drainage would be very fast, leaving them quite dry at times. To match their natural environment, you'll need to add grit to their compost to speed the passage of water through the pot. Others, such as *Griselinia littoralis*, prefer deeper soil and more moisture.

Sedums and sempervivums will survive just about anywhere. Their leaves are incredibly tough and resistant to periods of drought and salt-laden winds.

Don't forget

In any windy site, it's vital that you avoid tall plants and containers that could be blown over in gusty conditions.

Plants for windy sites

Aucuba japonica (spotted laurel)
Bellis perennis (daisy)
Calluna vulgaris (heather)
Caragana arborescens (pea tree)
Cordyline australis (New Zealand cabbage palm)
Erica (heaths)
Eryngium (sea holly)
Escallonia
Euonymus fortunei (spindle)
Geranium
Griselinia littoralis
Hebe
Helichrysum italicum
Mahonia aquifolium (Oregon grape)
Olearia × haastii
Osmanthus × burkwoodii
Phormium
Rosa rugosa (hedgehog rose)
Santolina chamaecyparissus
Sedum
Sempervivum (houseleeks)
Taxus baccata (common yew)

Balconies and roof terraces

Of all the places to create a garden, a balcony or roof terrace must be among the most challenging, particularly if it's windy and/or exposed to intense sun. It's worth persevering though, because your balcony will be a welcome haven when you sit and relax at the end of a busy day amid greenery instead of bricks and concrete. If you make full use of lush foliage, climbing and trailing plants and fragrant flowers, you can develop a secret world away from the surrounding activity. You can even control how much you're overlooked, by the strategic placing of a screen, windbreak or trellis.

The main restricting factor on a balcony is weight. Before you start, it may be worth consulting a structural engineer to see how much weight your balcony or roof can hold.

A medium-sized plastic container, when planted and watered, can weigh around 9kg (20lb) and you're likely to want more than one, so you need to choose your containers carefully: plastic, resin and wood are all lighter than concrete or ceramic. Loamless composts are lighter than loam-based, but they do dry out more quickly so you may need to add water-retaining crystals to the compost (*see* page 29). If you need to improve drainage in a pot, consider polystyrene packing chips rather than gravel in the base. If you're putting down a surface to walk on, bear in mind that thin, wooden decking is both light and warm to walk on and weighs less than tiles or slabs.

Additional precautions

The unpredictable nature of the weather around a building means that there are extra safety precautions you must take when you're gardening on a balcony or roof. All containers must be firmly secured against a random gust of wind, or there is a very real danger one may fall off and cause serious harm. The plants nearest the sides need particular attention and may need securing with brackets and chains. Never place pots on walls unless they're fenced off. Keep fire exits, doors and stairways clear of obstructions in case of emergency.

Don't forget

Make sure that any pots on the balcony can drain freely without the excess water raining down on anyone else's balcony.

Even in the heart of the city you can create a miniature haven for plants.
① Fresh herbs make an attractive, edible display on a sunny, sheltered roof garden.
② A raised metal planter and a pergola covered in a grapevine enliven the view.

Hot spots

A sheltered spot facing the sun during the day is likely to be very hot in summer. A major advantage of this is that you can grow certain container plants outdoors that would normally require a much warmer climate and/or protection elsewhere. The downside is that plants use up the available water very quickly and a lot of the water you apply can be lost to evaporation. Leaf scorch may also be a problem, so provide some overhead shade if you can.

A group of sun-lovers, including cannas, brugmansias, pelargoniums, dahlias and astelias, thrives in a hot spot. The hosta enjoys the shelter and shade provided by its neighbours.

Choosing plants

If you can't provide shade, make sure you choose the right plants for this sort of situation. As a rule, avoid plants with large, soft leaves (they'll burn easily). Look for silver, small or succulent leaves, or choose plants from hot climates such as the Mediterranean region, where they've adapted to dealing with bright, sunny conditions. Many herbs, such as thyme and rosemary, cope well in a very hot spot (where they smell especially wonderful because the heat speeds the evaporation of their volatile oils).

Choice of container

The heat of the sun will fall on the container as well as the plant, so it's important to choose your pot carefully. A metal pot will heat up extremely quickly and stay hot for a long time. This heat will damage a plant's roots, adversely affecting its growth. Pots made of natural, thick terracotta and ceramic materials are slower to heat, and they remain porous, so there's air movement through the sides, allowing the heat to escape. Unfortunately, water can also escape through the sides and evaporate, so you'll need to keep on top of your watering. Plastic pots are a compromise, because they heat up less than metal (although more than terracotta or ceramic) and they retain moisture for longer. The newer resin containers can often be better still, as the thicker construction means they're slower to adapt to the outside temperature.

Water

Water evaporates very quickly in a warm situation, so it's important to slow this down and keep what water there is available to the plants for the longest possible time. Water-retaining crystals (*see* page 29) can be added to the compost as you plant the container (*see* pages 32–6). A thick mulch over the surface of the compost will help to prevent evaporation directly from the compost, as well as reducing the chance of weeds germinating and competing for water (*see* page 30). Grouping plants together means that they can shade each other's roots. The leaves also form a canopy, which traps evaporated moisture and creates a microclimate of higher humidity, which in turn reduces the stress on the plants in hot conditions.

You can make watering much easier by installing a watering system for your 'hottest' containers, to deliver water directly into the container where it is most needed (*see* pages 46–7). The simplest system uses a plastic delivery pipe connected to the tap, with thin tubes that push into it as required and deliver water through a dripper nozzle into the pot. You can adjust the flow at each dripper so that each plant gets as much as it needs. You can even set it on a timer so that the water is applied overnight.

Plants for hot spots

Acacia dealbata (wattle)
Agave americana
Albizia julibrissin (silk tree)
Brugmansia
Callistemon citrinus (crimson bottlebrush)
Hedychium (ginger lilies)
Lagerstroemia indica (crepe flower)
Lavandula (lavender)
Sedum
Trachelospermum jasminoides (star jasmine)

Shady sites

Shade varies, from the deep shade cast by a building to the light, dappled shade cast by a small tree. Provided the area beneath is in light or moderate shade, you should be able to grow a wide variety of container plants, particularly woodland species.

Plants for shade

Some plants cope with shade better than others. Generally, most plants with dark green or large leaves should grow happily in a moderately shady site. This is because darker foliage contains more chlorophyll, which absorbs light energy, and leaves that have a large surface area can gather light more efficiently.

Choosing plants for deep shade is more difficult, because all plants need light for photosynthesis, the process by which plants make sugars and starches required for growth and energy, and when there is little or no sunlight this cannot take place. For such situations you need to think of the forest floor or lowest level of undergrowth in a natural situation, where the plants are used to coping with low light levels. Shrubs such as Christmas box (*Sarcococca confusa*) and *Viburnum davidii* will survive in these conditions, together with some ferns. Those that are particularly good for containers in deep shade include *Dryopteris filix-mas*, *Polypodium vulgare* 'Cornubiense' and *Polystichum setiferum*.

Be aware that in low light conditions, white- or yellow-variegated plants can revert to green (*see* page 52).

Many plants grow happily in pots in dappled shade, including the exotic chusan palm (*Trachycarpus fortunei*), hellebores and some grasses.

Drainage

Rapid moisture loss isn't going to be a problem in a shady spot. In fact, you may have the opposite problem: excess dampness building up and causing moss or algae to colonize the area. You can't force the water to disappear, but you can control this to some extent by making sure that all your containers can drain fairly quickly and that the water drains away completely, rather than collecting on the surface. It may help to add grit or sharp sand to the compost in the container, or to put a layer of grit in the base of each pot to speed the drainage.

Choice of container

In a cool, shady situation, the choice of container is not limited by heat or evaporation considerations. However, bear in mind that when light levels are low, a dark container is difficult to see. Light-coloured or shiny metal containers are highly visible, and they also help to reflect light (which can help the plants). Mulching the surface of the compost with glass pebbles is

Plants for shade

Aucuba japonica (spotted laurel)
Camellia
Dicentra spectabilis (bleeding heart)
Fatsia japonica (false castor oil)
Helleborus (hellebores)
Hosta
Mahonia aquifolium (Oregon grape)
Rhododendron
Sarcococca confusa (Christmas box)
Skimmia japonica
Viburnum davidii

also a good way of increasing light reflection. Unlike in a sunny site, where you need to group plants to retain moisture and create shade, in a shady place plants need all the light they can get. So don't layer your planting, or the ones beneath won't get any light at all. Instead, opt for a large, striking specimen plant in a container to make an eye-catching focal point on its own.

Urban gardens

Growing container plants in a town or city brings its own set of requirements. Pollution, privacy and security are generally more important in urban areas than they would be in a rural setting. Whatever problems there may be, they are more than offset by the benefits of coming home to your own little green oasis after a day spent amid the harsh landscape of the city.

Big tubs of bold-leaved and spiky architectural plants, including bamboos, hostas and acers, create a lush, larger-than-life, jungle-like effect in a small urban backyard.

Pollution-tolerant plants

Living in a built-up area can be hazardous for container plants, because they have to contend with fumes from car exhausts, salt from winter road treatments and people who knock them or push rubbish into them. Dust can form a coating on the leaves of plants, reducing their ability to photosynthesize food. If you do find that a coating is building up on the leaves, simply wipe them with a soft, damp cloth or spray them over with a hose.

Only the toughest and thorniest plants are likely to survive in busy, polluted cities, so look for plants with tough leaves such as hollies (*Ilex aquifolium*), *Skimmia japonica*, *Elaeagnus* and *Berberis*, or resilient plants such as the butterfly bush (*Buddleja davidii*), *Weigela florida* or *Forsythia*, which will survive almost anywhere. The attraction of tough, waxy leaves is that debris that accumulates on the surface washes off in the rain. *Amelanchier larmarckii*, mock orange (*Philadelphus*), *Cotoneaster* and *Leycesteria formosa* can also withstand the rigours of city living and still flower beautifully. Some plants such as *Olearia* × *haastii* and *Osmanthus* × *burkwoodii* have very small leaves and a dense habit so, even if the dirt builds up on part of the plant, the rest can still function. You can liven up the front of your house with a flowering quince (*Chaenomeles*), which will flower very early in the year and will grow happily against a trellis in a polluted area.

Berberis is the perfect city plant: it is relatively resistant to pollution and its spiny leaves discourage vandalism.

Security and privacy

It can be difficult to keep unwanted visitors off the garden, particularly if it's on a main road. People can damage your plants, either by thoughtless actions or vandalism. Theft of containers is also an issue in some areas. Most theft is opportunistic rather than planned, so reducing the things that can be easily carried off will help. For instance, fitting a small lock and chain to your hanging basket and putting a brick in the base of a large container to make it heavier will help. Grow prickly plants such as *Rosa rugosa* in containers that are outside your property, and use low trellis in long, rectangular containers to make a physical boundary to your property to discourage people from using it as a short cut. Install security lighting that comes on if someone approaches, because they're less likely to steal in the full glare of a light.

If lack of privacy is an issue in an urban garden, consider installing a screen or trellis, which will also act as a windbreak and protect plants (*see* pages 16–17 and 117).

Almost any small, enclosed space surrounded by buildings or walls could be classed as a courtyard. The great practical advantage of having a courtyard is that the walls retain heat and so it tends to be warmer and more sheltered than surrounding areas, making it a good environment for growing container plants that would struggle in a cooler position or if exposed to wind.

Depending on the alignment of the surrounding buildings, your courtyard may be in shade all day long or in full sun for part of the day and shade for the rest. It's important to have the right plants in the right part of the area so that the shade-tolerant plants aren't scorched and the sun-lovers don't become leggy and drawn in the shade.

Good plants for courtyards
Plants that you could try in a courtyard that gets some sun during the day include *Acacia*, *Clianthus puniceus* and *Trachelospermum asiaticum*, which you can train against a wall, *Citrus* and *Ensete ventricosum*, with their ornamental fruits, and *Lantana camara*, *Callistemon citrinus*, *Lagerstroemia indica* and the lavender *Lavandula stoechas*, with their stunning flowers. Some of these plants, such as the *Trachelospermum asiaticum*, will look good over winter provided the site is sheltered, but most will need to be moved indoors in case of frost, because they originate from warmer climates. If your courtyard gets very little or no sun at all, you'll need to use shade-loving plants, such as camellias, *Fatsia japonica*, hellebores and ferns.

Creating a sense of space
The key to success in a small, contained area such as a courtyard is to make it seem bigger while retaining the intimate feeling of enclosure and privacy. One of the secrets is to soften the surrounding stark, hard lines of the building with climbing plants in pots, so that you lose a firm point of reference. You could paint the wall dark green to create a natural-looking backdrop for plants, or white to increase light levels and make the space seem bigger. You can also achieve this by using mirrors and choosing pale-coloured containers and covering the ground with pale gravel.

An outdoor room
A courtyard can be treated as an extension to the house. Because it's sheltered, it's the ideal place for a seating area. Its proximity to the building's mains electricity supply means that installing lighting is a relatively straightforward business. In effect a courtyard – more than any other ground-level outdoor space – has the potential to become an outdoor room in the true sense.

From a design point of view, a courtyard often presents a great opportunity to experiment and create an entirely different style or mood from the rest of the garden.

Container plants bring a courtyard to life and set the style and ambience.
① Lush planting, wall pots, and a water feature in a clay jar create an exotic feel.
② Trimmed box balls strike a more classic note and a mirror set in the trellis makes the shady area appear larger and brighter.

Index

Page numbers in *italics* refer to plants illustrated and/or described in the 'Plants for Containers' chapter.

Acknowledgements

BBC and Outhouse would like to thank the following for their assistance in preparing this book: Andrew McIndoe for his advice and guidance; Helena Caldon for picture research; Lindsey Brown for proofreading; June Wilkins for the index; Dan Whiting of Ball Colegrave Ltd for his invaluable help in providing photographs.

Picture credits

Key t = top; b = bottom; l = left; r = right; c = centre

All photographs by Jonathan Buckley except the following:

Ball Colegrave 92tl; 92bl; 93bl; 93tr; 94br

Benary Ltd 83tc; 86tl

GAP Photos Pernilla Baghdahl 75tc; Mark Bolton 73tc; Torie Chugg 79tr; FhF Greenmedia 76tr(r); Jerry Harpur 91tr; Gerald Majumdar 73bl; Fiona McLeod 83bl; Visions 93br; Juliette Wade 96tc; Kit Young 71br

The Garden Collection Torie Chugg 94tc; Liz Eddison 15, 23tr, 23br, 24(2), 35l, 36, 40, 41, 43r, 123(1); Derek Harris 91bl; Andrew Lawson 23tl, 81(2), 85br, 86bl; Gary Rogers 13(1); Jane Sebire 19(2); Nicola Stocken Tomkins 24(1), 30(2, 3), 35r, 43l, 67r, 101tc; Neil Sutherland 27

Garden Picture Library Photolibrary Group 82bc, 101tl, 101bc, 101br

Garden World Images 75tr; 93bc; M. Hughes-Jones 77bc; 87br; 89bc; G. Smith 98bc

Antonia Gordon 119(1)

Andrew McIndoe 13(2), 30(1), 37(1, 3), 68bc, 70tl, 70tc, 70br, 71bl, 72bl, 72bc, 73tl, 73bc, 73br, 75bl, 76tc, 76bc, 79bl, 80br, 82tc, 83tl, 88tl, 91tc, 92br, 96bc

Nature Photographers Ltd Paul Sterry 85bc

Raymond Turner 42, 122(tr)

Thanks are also due to the following designers and owners whose gardens appear in the book:

Maureen Allen 17; Lesley Bremness 41; Gill Brown 11bl, 16, 19t; Zoe Cain 118; Alan Capper 21(3); Fergus Garrett 18; Diarmuid Gavin 119(2); Anthony Goff 25(4), 63; Robin Green & Ralph Cade 20, 116, 120; Jeffery Hewitt 15; Jim Honey & James Dyson 21(1); Paul Kelly 12bl; Virginia Kennedy 12br; Carol Klein 113b; Rani Lall 117; Christopher Lloyd, Great Dixter 8, 22, 48, 108tr; John Massey, Ashwood Nurseries 26, 55tr, 115; Jackie McLaren 123(2); Peter Niczewski 121; Pots and Pithoi 23tl; Faith Raven 52; Sarah Raven, Perch Hill 2–3, 10, 14, 102, 107; Gill Siddell 110t; Sue and Wol Staines, Glen Chantry 66; Georgina Steeds 23tr; Carole Vincent 9, 21(2); Andrew Walker 123(1)